Praise for *They Call You Back*

"With his deeply personal *They Call You Back*, Tim Z. Hernandez completes an ambitious and essential trilogy that has helped redefine the history of California's Central Valley, and of the Mexican and Mexican American farmworkers who labor there. Haunting and beautiful, these works will stay with you long after you have read the last page."

—HÉCTOR TOBAR, AUTHOR OF *OUR MIGRANT SOULS*

"Hernandez takes us on a poignant, eye-opening journey of self-discovery and historical insights, leading to interesting revelations and hard truths. A beautifully written story full of layers and complexities."

—REYNA GRANDE, AUTHOR OF *A BALLAD OF LOVE AND GLORY*

"Tim Z. Hernandez is one of the most soulful witnesses of our time. He doesn't just voyage to the end of the earth for his stories, he steps beyond—invoking the spirits as he follows the blood. *They Call You Back* is the genesis of his artistry, as riveting as it is necessary."

—STEPHANIE ELIZONDO GRIEST, AUTHOR OF *ALL THE AGENTS AND SAINTS*

"Tim Z. Hernandez is on a quest. Through the lucid clarity of his transcendent prose, he is searching for the resolution of a tragedy and its players. But by transforming a forgotten news story into a vital living document, he is transforming us into the 'storykeepers' of our own myth."

—OCTAVIO SOLIS, AUTHOR OF *RETABLOS*

"Tim Z. Hernandez's brilliance in *They Call You Back* is his keen eye as a master storyteller. He writes with precision and clarity, passionately and elegantly, to connect a haunting past with an unsettling future. *They Call You Back* transforms life into history, unfolding dark family secrets that linger in the collective memory of generations . . . a memoir that is as generous and humble as the people he brings back to life with his extraordinary words. Vivid prose, powerful read!"

—ALFREDO CORCHADO, AUTHOR OF *MIDNIGHT IN MEXICO* AND *HOMELANDS*

"In this brilliant Joycean work of memoir—the site being the agricultural Central Valley of California where white power dominates the majority of brown people—poet Tim Z. Hernandez tells stories within stories reflecting the trauma experienced in this setting that fuels both his passion and vulnerabilities."

—ROXANNE DUNBAR-ORTIZ, AUTHOR OF *NOT A 'NATION OF IMMIGRANTS': SETTLER COLONIALISM, WHITE SUPREMACY, AND A HISTORY OF ERASURE AND EXCLUSION*

"In this shameful moment, as politicians, conservative pundits, and agenda-driven 'concerned citizen' groups endeavor to suppress the complexities of our nation's history, Tim Z. Hernandez's writing and its stalwart resistance to erasure proves not only timely but urgent. *They Call You Back* delivers a stunning rebuke to those who would deny the past and set us on an inexorable path to repeat its atrocities."

—LORRAINE M. LÓPEZ, AUTHOR OF *THE DARLING*

"This is a story of the haunting of the living and the dead and the complicated and terrifying ways we deal with our trauma of living in a world of subjugated stories, lost voices, familial, sometimes our own, and the writer's search to make sense of it all. In the beginning and end, this is a book that struggles and at times reconciles with what it means to live in a world where 'they' shape our sleep, our breath, our daily routine. It reveals the constant struggle of holding 'them' at bay and realizing that we were 'they' all along."

—JOHN-MICHAEL RIVERA, AUTHOR OF *UNDOCUMENTS*

THEY CALL YOU BACK

Camino del Sol
A Latinx Literary Series
Rigoberto González, Series Editor

TIM Z. HERNANDEZ

THEY CALL YOU BACK

A Lost History, A Search, A Memoir

THE UNIVERSITY OF
ARIZONA PRESS
TUCSON

The University of Arizona Press
www.uapress.arizona.edu

We respectfully acknowledge the University of Arizona is on the land and territories of Indigenous peoples. Today, Arizona is home to twenty-two federally recognized tribes, with Tucson being home to the O'odham and the Yaqui. Committed to diversity and inclusion, the University strives to build sustainable relationships with sovereign Native Nations and Indigenous communities through education offerings, partnerships, and community service.

ISBN-13: 978-0-8165-5361-7 (hardcover)
ISBN-13: 978-0-8165-5362-4 (ebook)

Cover design by Leigh McDonald
Cover photo of Tim Z. Hernandez courtesy of the author
Designed and typeset by Leigh McDonald in Bell MT Std 11/14 and Rift (display)

Note: Only a few names have been changed, and in one case redacted upon the family's request, for the purpose of protecting the identities of individuals. This account is true to my recollection of events, my own memory, and my own research, and true to the families who lived it and whose testimonies I used to generate this narrative. In instances where I have written reenactments, it is not merely for fiction's sake, but rather to create a believable, and as close to actual, rendering based on my firsthand knowledge of and expertise on this subject, records, documents, newspaper articles, interviews with individuals, and eyewitness testimony. In this way, these passages should be looked at strictly as a reenactment, and not as fictional.

Library of Congress Cataloging-in-Publication Data
Names: Hernandez, Tim Z., author.
Title: They call you back : a lost history, a search, a memoir / Tim Z. Hernandez.
Other titles: Camino del sol.
Description: Tucson : University of Arizona Press, 2024. | Series: Camino del sol: a Latinx literary series | Includes bibliographical references.
Identifiers: LCCN 2024000591 (print) | LCCN 2024000592 (ebook) | ISBN 9780816553617 (hardcover) | ISBN 9780816553624 (ebook)
Subjects: LCSH: Hernandez, Tim Z. | Aircraft accident victims' families. | Deportees—Family relationships. | Aircraft accidents—California—Diablo Range. | Disaster justice.
Classification: LCC PS3608.E768 Z46 2024 (print) | LCC PS3608.E768 (ebook) | DDC 813/.6 [B]—dc23/eng/20240419
LC record available at https://lccn.loc.gov/2024000591
LC ebook record available at https://lccn.loc.gov/2024000592

Printed in the United States of America
♾ This paper meets the requirements of ANSI/NISO Z39.48-1992 (Permanence of Paper).

CONTENTS

AUTHOR'S NOTE

I SEARCH FOR PEOPLE. No, I am not a detective, nor have I ever been schooled in investigations of any kind. I'm just a soul for whom curiosity is not a plaything but a haunting. Once I'm pinpricked by the unknown, I must go seeking answers. In one of its earliest forms, the word *obsession* was yoked with the Latin *obsideo*—to be held captive by spirits. A description that feels not too far off the mark for me. This bleeds into my life in big and small ways. It takes a herculean effort for me to not act upon every question life throws my way. I've seen therapists for it, but they've assured me it's not a condition. Inherently, this work of searching for people requires that I obsess. It demands that I scrutinize the same roads, repeatedly, over a span of years. The physical roads as much as the psychological ones, but especially the spiritual ones. And it is with this in mind that I've assembled the stories, images, and testimonies included here. Not as a linear road map of where I've been or what I've done, but instead as a series of intersecting stories, braided together to convey not just *how* I went about these searches, but, more importantly, *why*. Throughout, you'll find only a slight consideration of chronology for context. Not unlike a map with nothing but the letter *N* in the legend for reference. Either way, fate always assures we arrive at our destination.

"The worst airplane disaster in California's history." Los Gatos Canyon, 1948.

They're coming, more and more, they're coming.
But when they come they are never simply they,
they are a face, a smile, eyes unlike any others,
there is no they when they come.

—CHARLES BOWDEN, *SONATA*

THEY

January 29, 2018, California State Senate

THEY WANT TO KNOW where it all began. They ask questions and then stare at you for answers. They are relentless. When your response doesn't come quick enough, they look at you strangely, curiously. They're reporters and politicians, used to quick answers, witty remarks. They ask you again, "What made you want to go searching for the survivors of the plane crash?" You've never been good at veiling your emotions. "Yes, tell us how this all got started." You've fielded these questions a thousand times. But what makes this time different is that it's the seventieth anniversary of the plane crash at Los Gatos, and you're standing in the State Capitol building in Sacramento, California, invited here to rectify the historical injustice that occurred long ago. An incident that took the lives of thirty-two passengers, twenty-eight of them Mexican nationals, bracero workers who were being sent home but never made it. Their bodies dumped into an unmarked mass grave, "the largest in California's history." A year ago, you published a book, *All They Will Call You*, about the seven families you'd found so far. But that was just the beginning. There are still twenty-one more out there. How did it all get started? The truth is it began with them—the media. When, in 1948, they omitted the names of the Mexican passengers and opted instead to tag twenty-eight human beings with the label of "deportees." But you remind yourself that this is supposed to be a celebratory moment. The red flashing lights of their recording devices pull you back.

They want to hear from you. They're growing impatient. You decide that this moment calls for an honesty as unapologetic as the wound itself. The time for ready-made responses is over. Early on you simply said, "It was an injustice, and somebody needed to right this wrong." But these are senators and congressmen, people seasoned in the art of bullshit, and you want no part of it. A day as meaningful and symbolic as this demands only the truth, no matter how complex. The truth? That there are several ways to answer this question, several "beginnings" to this journey.

"Then give us just one," a reporter replies, chuckling. They all nod.

"One?" Okay then—

࿊

They arrive in the middle of the night. Sometimes one, but lately more. I'm in a deep sleep when suddenly my eyes slam open. I'm fully conscious and can't speak or move, but I can see everything. My bedroom is lit in crimson light. Still and silent. Everything is in its place. And then it approaches. Not visible at first, more of an intuitive feeling. I want to react but I'm completely immobile. Some call this sleep paralysis. But knowing its name doesn't lessen the weight that bears down on my body in this moment. It doesn't make it any less real. My neck and jaw feel like they're made of concrete, and I can't lift my arms, much less sit up. This is when the ball of light emerges. It drifts toward me. What I'm telling you about is actually happening. It isn't a dream. I'm wide awake and there's a fist-size white light hovering over me. I try to speak, but instead a growl slips from my mouth. The first time the light appeared I was twenty-one, and my uncle had just been killed. When it hovered over me, I forced his name out of my throat—*Virgil!*—and it shot through the wall.

But lately they've come to me whole, fully formed. Lately there is no ball of light. And they arrive together. The last time, they appeared in my bedroom. And unlike before, I wasn't paralyzed. I was woken up by the sound of spoons tinkling in ceramic cups, and boots walking on my hardwood floor. When my eyes opened, all four of them were near my closet, which had turned into a small kitchen. They were staring at me: two men, two women. "Se despertó," one of the women said. One of the men leaned toward me. He was tall, at least six feet, and wore a brown fedora and dirty white shirt. They were all dressed in dated attire. The air around them was light, as if they had just been laughing, anticipating my arrival. I wasn't afraid. Not this time. I gathered myself to speak and quickly sat up in bed, but when I did, it startled them and they vanished. I turned the bedside lamp on. I knew what I'd seen. I got out of bed and hurried to catch them slipping out the front door of my house. I opened it and found myself standing at the top of the stairs, alone, in the cold February night. I stared across the rooftops at the distant floodlights that came from the wall that stitches together El Paso, Ciudad Juárez, and New Mexico—a braid of my three ancestral homelands. I was trying to understand why they would enter my room only to wake me and then rush off. What were they trying to tell me? The stars glimmered above this part of the desert, and once again I felt duped. I returned to my room, opened my journal, and wrote: *Has all this gotten to me? Am I beyond obsession? Where's the line? The apparitions and this compulsive need to document every part of the search . . . but it's the only way I know to make sense of it . . . writing, audio, photographs, I must record everything. A trail of crumbs to find my way back . . .*

In the weeks following the event at the State Capitol, I try describing in words what took place, but my attempts are flimsy. Maybe it requires more distance, I tell myself. What occurred was so surreal that I'm wary of my own version of events. In the following months, I discover various media reports that also attempt to convey the details of that day on the Senate floor. In reference to my search, some will write, *It's his life's work.* And it's this line alone that nags me. I find it offensive, and I can't let it go. Sure, reporters are only human after all, but the stories we write have the potential to outlast us all. So permit me to correct this here and now. To call it "my work" is inaccurate. It assumes that the interest of this story is purely my own. As if it's been a unilateral decision to spend the last thirteen years of my life searching for the surviving family of the unknown victims of what came to be known as "the worst plane crash in California's history." But this is only a fragment of the truth. Let me set the record straight. I assure you in every way, this search has come from both sides of the astral plane. There is, in fact, the other side. *Their* side. The victims themselves, who have the greatest investment in my search. It's *they* who've been lost to their families for over seven decades now. It's *they* who are still the source of immense grief in the hearts of those who loved them, many of whom still live and walk among us. And it's *their* families who stand to benefit from my search. It's simply too easy to forget—and at times I have—that this is not *my* story. This is *their* story. And I'm but one minor character inside of it. For *they* too speak. *They* too have their say in the matter. *They*, the anonymous spirits, who for almost a century have existed only in the quiet margins reserved for ghosts and memories of the disappeared.

And they continue to find me. In dreams and in the flesh, they come. And in the very alive eyes and faces of their descendants, their brothers and sisters, grandchildren, and great-grandchildren, in whom you can see them still breathing. And they come to me in the objects they carried, in the ephemera, through which they've communicated clues directly to me, whispered in my ear secrets they were too modest to share with even their own family. Evidence of their journey, and of what took place in the months and days leading up to that fateful morning of January 28, 1948. In some cases I can hear their voices clearly. So clearly that I can tell you how in the final days before twenty-year-old Alberto Raigoza Carlos was killed, there was an innocent quality in his voice, a kind of timid undertone as he penned his last words to his sister Carlota from a boarding house in Salinas, California: *Please Carlota, let me know if Daniel is coming back to Salinas*... Three weeks later he'd be burned alive in the plane crash at Los Gatos.

You might think I'm exaggerating with all this talk of ghosts, or that I'm being metaphorical, but you're wrong. I'm telling you they come to me. At all hours, at any given moment, they come. But what exactly they are communicating, and why, are the questions I have pondered for more than a decade now. What is it I have not yet grasped? In what dark corners have I dared not probe? Whose silences have I not yet recorded? To record and to remember (in Spanish *recordar*) share a root word: *recordis*—to pass back through the heart. Permit me to pass back through. In this, my thirteenth year of an exhaustive search, the only thing clear is that this story is not finished with me. They are not finished with me. They have more to teach me—to teach us. And they will not stop until every last one of them has had their say. They will not let us go. They call you back.

For my grandparents, sanemos juntos—

Estela Constante, Felix Hernandez, Magdalena Maynes, Alejandro Zuñiga Sr.

THEY CALL YOU BACK

I

THE ORIGIN STORIES

I was simply trying to recover what had been lost, to return to the first home, to get back the rapture of first love.

—BELL HOOKS, *ALL ABOUT LOVE*

1

A BEGINNING

Socorro, New Mexico, 1958

HE'S AT THE BACK of the house, huddled over a pile of mesquite wood. A small fire at his feet. It's frigid out. Snow's coming in. Fall's begun falling. The peaks of Mount Magdalena were dusted white last night. She stands behind him, witnessing. She can see plumes of breath unfurling around his head. She's a child, barely five. She's watching him work. Her father. Short sighs escape his mouth. With a handsaw he's cutting wood. His body heaves up and down. His nose drips and he wipes it on his sleeve. Keeps sawing. When he's done, he pulls the small box that he's constructing toward him. Gets down on his knees, in the dirt. Warms his hands over the fire. He takes the freshly cut piece of wood and begins to hammer it to the box. A lid for the coffin. The coffin is small, three feet long at most. It's shaped like a rectangle. Not like a coffin at all. But it's a coffin. She approaches her father as he hammers away. He senses her, stops and turns. "Go back in the house, Chita," he says. Chita stays for a moment. Her body trembles in the cold. "Go." In a second, Chita will follow orders. But for a brief moment she stays put. Chita is petite, straight hair, big eyes. She is my mother. Though she doesn't know this yet. But if you look closely at her eyes you'll see that I'm already there. In that moment with her, trembling the same. She sees that her father's eyes are red. He's been crying. There are no tears visible. When Alejandro cries, rarely does it involve tears. It's just an expression on his face. Everything tightens. He becomes a vault from which nothing escapes. Alejandro returns to fitting the lid for the coffin. Chita knows who the coffin is for. The baby is still inside the house. Two days ago the baby didn't wake up. The baby wasn't an infant anymore, but he was still a baby. He had lived two years of his life. Long enough to make it hurt. His name was Humberto. But because he was a baby, they called him Betito.

Tomorrow they will bury Betito at the local camposanto, in the shadow of the mountain which bears my grandmother's name. It will be a small procession. Alejandro prefers it this way. Magdalena can't think straight, much less make decisions. Chita will walk with her family to the cemetery, though later she will vaguely remember any of it. They will dress Betito humbly, bundle him in his little blanket, place him in the small coffin, and carry him to the San Miguel Cemetery. The whole way, Magdalena, Chita, Hito, and the rest of their siblings, including baby Virgil, will cry. Or maybe they don't, but every time this story is told to me, I imagine they do. Alejandro will walk coldly in the direction of the mountain. They will arrive in the easternmost section of the San Miguel Cemetery, the area reserved for babies. There, my grandfather will use a spade to dig a small hole in the cold, compact earth. The padre will sprinkle holy water. A prayer will be said. My grandfather will place Betito's coffin down in the hole. He will shovel the earth back over it. In these moments words hold no power, so none are spoken. Magdalena and the kids will go home. Shortly after, so will my grandfather. But not before he places a wooden cross made of mesquite over the small mound. They will let go of Betito now. They will try and forget. But they never will. No one ever forgets. Over time, and due to the harsh conditions of the desert, the wood will weaken and disintegrate. In a matter of years, the cross will be no more. And then, years later, the wood will be pushed around by the monsoons. Before long, there'll be no way of ever tracing back their steps to find Betito. This is true. I know this, because many years later, Chita, a woman now with her own children, will return to that cemetery searching for her baby brother's grave. And she will bring me along, her only son, age eleven. Together my mother and I will search the unmarked graves, knowing it will take a miracle to find him. But we believe in miracles, so we search. Me in my fading blue Dodgers baseball cap and ripped jeans, my mother in her summer blouse and stringy hair. With only the wind and our silence to keep us company. This is how it exists in my memory, just Mom and me. We start at each end of the cemetery and work our way toward one another. A swath of land filled with dead people and history between us. Everything is a clue. Every stone imbued with meaning. We walk past half-buried shards of adobe and fragments of wood, and kneel down to lift up portions of the hard earth and let it sift through our fingers, hoping to find signs of Betito. Much later I will learn there is a word for this, "unearthing." It means that the earth reveals its secrets to those who pay attention. But I am new to this, and I am learning. Hours later, our mission of locating Betito's grave is unsuccessful. We go home empty-handed. So many questions left unanswered. So much mystery in my mother's silence.

This was the first search.

2

THE BUTTERFLY

IN THE DAYS immediately before (or immediately after) Betito's death, a white butterfly drifted into my grandmother Magdalena's kitchen. Alejandro, being from South Texas and therefore superstitious, was furious about it. He chased the ominous messenger around the house, shouting for Magdalena to help him "get the damn thing out!" Magdalena, being from New Mexico, and therefore practical, shook her head, not one to give weight to his irrational beliefs. But Alejandro was beyond reason. Growing up as a child in Roma, Texas, in the shadow of the Mexican border, he was aware that a butterfly in the house was a sign of death. Perhaps at that point Betito was not yet dead, but sick with pneumonia, and if Alejandro could usher away the creature then he could save the baby. Perhaps by then Betito was already dead and Alejandro needed something to blame. Or perhaps Alejandro sought to wield control over a situation in which he had none, as fathers will often do. Naturally, this story has holes in it, redactions of memory. What is curious, though, is Alejandro's impulse to not actually kill the wraith, but to escort it outside, away from the house, a display of reverence if there ever was one.

Chita doesn't actually remember what became of the butterfly. She only remembers that late that night, or in the predawn hours of morning, she heard a sound so disturbing that it forced her out of bed to search for the source. She followed the sound into the kitchen, and what she saw was more startling than what she had imagined. Seated at the table, buckled over in a chair, was Alejandro, sobbing. Unable to maintain his stoic façade any longer. The rash of bad luck that had been the last several years of their life was too much to bear. Chita watched her father cry like she'd never seen him cry before, while her mother Magdalena stood over him, cradling him like a baby, his head pressed against her left breast, which was now drenched in the salt of his grief.

Witnessing this made Chita nervous. She felt butterflies in her stomach. No, anything but butterflies, she thought. Moths perhaps. Or a fly. Yes, a fly. Such harmless creatures. Little did Chita know in that moment the degree of malice that a single fly is capable of. Though in time she'd come to learn.

୧

It was a known fact that my grandfather, skilled at shooting, hated guns. In fact, he was a notorious hater of many things. While in the Korean War he hated being at war. And then he hated returning home from the war. He hated the government for treating veterans, especially brown veterans, "like shit." My grandfather hated asking for help. And yet he had no choice. He hated administrators with their smug faces, who forgot your name seconds after you said it. He hated elevators, sterile buildings, and high-rises, preferring to be closer to the earth, for nothing can fall when it's close to the earth. My grandfather was self-reliant, tough, and resourceful. Traits he would never credit the military for. He didn't take more than his equal share because he hated cheaters and swindlers. Considered himself an honest man, honest to a fault. He had a vision of the world, and for his family, and in the early years he acted in accordance with that vision. His kids wanted toys, he'd teach them to make their own toys. They wanted candy, he'd teach them to make their own candy. He was DIY before DIY was cool. Teaching his kids every step of the way. Before reaching puberty, they knew how to harvest their own honey, kill and skin their own rabbits, and cobble their own busted shoes. Alejandro hated television, so they never had one. For entertainment he'd break out his harmonica, and he and Magdalena would teach the children to dance. It was a known fact that my grandparents were jitterbug champions in the late '40s when they lived in East Los Angeles, which is how my grandfather got his nickname,

"El Gusano," for the way he danced. All this before the arrival of the butterfly. And when Magdalena finally got sick with breast cancer, he hated that the nearest cancer specialist was in Galveston, Texas, which may as well have been Mars. But he drove her the eight hundred miles without a single complaint, for more than any other hate in the world, he would've hated losing Magdalena most. As their luck would have it, it was the year of Hurricane Abby, and the streets of Galveston were torrents, and in that moment only Alejandro could tell you how much he hated Mother Nature. He pulled up to the front of the hospital and lifted his ailing wife out of the car and carried her over the floodwaters and into the waiting room. They treated my grandmother by cutting her left breast out, and after several days released her, claiming there wasn't anything further they could do. Death was imminent. Alejandro hated the doctors and their dire prognosis. He laid Magdalena down in the back seat of the car and returned to Laredo, where they had been living in that brief hiccup of time. He hated the long road back. Each mile marker counting down the days like an hourglass. The hate in his gut gathering like a great dune of desert sand.

In July 1964, Alejandro sits down at the kitchen table to write a most difficult letter. Nena is barely conscious, he knows she's dying, and he's struggling to accept that once again death comes pounding its fist against their door. It's a letter to his sister-in-law, Apolonia, who lives in Deming, New Mexico. This is the final straw. You can hear it in his tone. Since they first fell in love they have had three babies die: Tilly #1, Betito, Roel. But there are still six babies that rely on them: Hito (13), Mom (11), Emily (9), Virgil (7), Tilly #2 (5), and baby Irma (1). Alejandro composes himself and writes the letter:

Mrs. Polly Casillas,

Nena is still sick from the illness. You can imagine how the children and I feel. And we have no one here to help us, except for Dios Nuestro Señor Jesucristo*. But this is God's will. Of course, my wish is to bring her to you, but that would require bringing all the children, and that would be a very uncomfortable situation. Polly, it hurts to tell you this, but she is very sick. Please let the family know. We send you and Ángel our regards, on behalf of myself, Nena, and all the children.*

With love, from those who appreciate you so much,
Alejandro Zuñiga

The illness. My grandpa can't bring himself to write it. Cancer. And even though they've cut it out, it's already spread through her body. He's in no condition to raise six children alone, he knows this. You can sense this in his words. He sees it coming. They all do.

One day Chita is left alone to care for her mother, which includes washing her wound periodically with a solution of warm water and salt. She does as told. But the wound is badly infected, and when she goes to clean it she sees a small worm wiggle out from between the stitches in her skin. A maggot. When she wasn't paying attention a fly had perched itself there and laid its egg. Chita brushes it off, but she's afraid it's too late. And she's right. Days later Nena dies, and by the next morning Alejandro will have taken to drinking until he blacks out— his only consolation. Chita will grow up wondering if this was all her fault.

And those were the good times.

But now comes the bad. My grandfather has lost the glue that held him together, made him whole—Magdalena. Their first child stillborn. Their second child lost to crib death. And Betito, buried now in some forgotten camposanto in a desert town whose very name means "to wail." Gone are the days when he would drag home a fallen branch and whittle toys for the children, or when he would play harmonica for them, or when they gathered honey from the mesquite tree. That father is a distant memory. People in town know he's a widower. They refer to his children as huérfanos, orphans. His PTSD from the war haunts him. A car backfires and he dives under a table. Hisses as he crawls out from underneath it. Now Alejandro roams Deming aimlessly, alone.

One drunken night he returns home in a rage. The children scramble away from the house, their hands interlinked so no one gets left behind. In his blackout, he grabs his rifle, hollers for them to come back, fires shots at the night sky. The stars become bullet holes. And this is now routine. On one night they hide in the alleyway behind their adobe house. More shots, more stars appear. On another night they hide under the overpass of Interstate 10. Nights like these put the fear of God in Chita, who is twelve by now. And where she goes, so do I, and so the fear of God is mine too. Her brother Hito calms us. He calms all his siblings. Especially the youngest,

Virgil. He is trembling. "Where's Irma?" In their haste they left baby Irma in the house. They worry Alejandro will hurt her. Hours later there is silence. They see the house lights are all off. They tiptoe back inside and find their father out cold, baby Irma asleep in her bassinet. This is their life now. Alejandro is volatile and erratic, exacerbated by alcohol's grip. Nothing is ever certain again. The gravitational pull of their once family has stopped, and there's nothing to keep their feet planted. From here they'll hold on to one another for as long as they can, until one by one they slip and go drifting in opposite directions. No longer the magnetic force of their mother's love to hold them together, to keep them as one unit, to remind them that they were all born from one single womb, into one single life, with one single blood. Never no more, again.

When Alejandro wakes up he will notice another child missing. Little by little, the six lives who once made up his entire world will be no more. The hate grows over his shoulders and face, and by the time it takes hold of him completely he's in a VA hospital bed, alone, in Tucson, Arizona. The nurse tells him his situation is dire, he should contact his children. "I have no children," he says. And this is how Chita finds him. Near death, bleeding internally, denying love. In their final moments together he has no words for her. Only bitter silence. An overwhelming fire consumes her—her only inheritance. And now this too becomes my inheritance.

3

VIRGIL

Summer, 1984

IT COMES TO ME like an old family video without sound. Virgil is standing in the parking lot of the Balboa Motel, in the middle of Deming. His chest out, defiant, a broad smile on his face. He is now twenty-seven years old, desert-stricken, with a bronze aura, and unapologetically beautiful. His skin is like raw suede, and his curly hair is slicked back by its natural oils, and he smells like a chaparral minutes after a hard rain. He has on denim pants and a plain white tank top, exposing his sun-kissed arms and collarbone. Leather work boots, and a brown leather belt that holds a small knife sheath. Black aviator sunglasses that, when removed, leave the shadow of his tan. This is his only adornment. No jewelry. No pretense. He's a desert Adonis, young and experienced. He stares out beyond the dry desolate land like a coyote whose eyes have seen every den and cliff that this terrain has put in his way. He drops his cigarette into the sand and smudges it with his work boot. And then he looks at me, as if he's seen me before, as if he knows me. In this moment, I am ten years old, and enamored.

There's a peculiar affection a boy feels for an uncle, even an uncle he has never before met but has only been told about in stories. Especially then. Because up until the moment they meet, the uncle is in every way mythical to the boy's mind. And the boy can't help but visualize this man, invent the attributes, the shape of his persona, how he walks, the way he talks or laughs or just stands perfectly still in the desert air. Especially when that boy was gifted the ability to visualize with great clarity any image that enters his mind's eye. Which is to say, long before I had ever met Virgil, I had already forged a deep connection with him.

That summer we drove from central California to New Mexico specifically to find Virgil. My mom had heard that her baby brother was going through some rough times back in Deming, and that was enough reason to go looking for him. The sense of responsibility for her younger siblings had never left. Years later, Virgil himself would express to Chita, "You're the only mother I ever knew." Trying to locate a man who'd been wandering the Southwest alone since he was a kid is a lesson in persistence.

We first stopped at the house of a relative, who directed us to another relative, who then told us check with Virgil's girlfriend, who worked at the nearby 7-Eleven. So we went to the 7-Eleven, where I got out of the car with my mom and went inside. I watched her ask the person behind the counter if so-and-so was working. She was. They called the woman out. She and my mom exchanged information. She pointed my mom to a nearby hotel. We got back in the car, where my dad and little sister Dee were waiting, and then drove over to a small pink motel in the center of town. I went with my mom to the front office and watched as she asked for a guest named Virgil Zuñiga. A few minutes later we were knocking on a room door. A gust of sand blowing against our eyes. My mom told me to go wait in the car. From there I could see the motel room door open. A man stepped out and immediately threw his arms around my mom. It lasted several minutes. Virgil.

While the adults stood around catching up, Dee and I were in the swimming pool, cooling off from the desert heat. At one point, as I waded in the shallow end, I found myself unable to take my eyes off of Virgil. Even at such a distance, he looked larger than life to me. I was enthralled by him. The subject of what they were discussing I would never know. I only know that whatever was said, at the end of it all my parents had convinced my uncle to come with us. Back to California. And so he did. Whatever sort of trouble Virgil was in, he was safe and cared for now. An idea took shape within me: to search and to love were synonymous.

From then on, I followed in my uncle's shadow. I began to dress like him. I asked my parents for boots like his. I wanted to own the desert the way he did. To walk this world unafraid as he did. To smoke cigarettes and have my skin scarred with fading tattoos bearing the names of people, those I loved and those who left. I wanted to know how to build things with my own hands. How to make men laugh out loud with my sharp wit when the time called for it. I took on his laugh. I can still hear it in me sometimes. His unconscious swagger. I prayed for curls.

This was the second search.

II

UNEARTHINGS

Storytellers seek the footprints of lost memory, love and pain, that cannot be seen but are never erased.

—EDUARDO GALEANO, *HUNTER OF STORIES*

4

A SYNCHRONISTIC MEETING

2018

I'M ON AN AIRPLANE, departing Fresno, California, for Fort Smith, Arkansas. Two rows behind me, I hear a woman mention the town of Visalia. No one ever mentions the town of Visalia—an inconspicuous patch, fifty miles southeast of Fresno, tucked at the foot of the Sierra Nevadas. It's where I attended high school, and where my parents still live to this day. It's unusual to hear the name fall from the lips of strangers, and when it does, rarely is it in good light. But Visalia has earned its reputation.

It began as a descendant of the South, named after Visalia, Kentucky. In the twenties it became a Klan hive, and if you inhale deep enough you can still smell the cotton sheets. A decade later it became the actual site that inspired John Steinbeck's horrific flood scene in *The Grapes of Wrath.* Ground zero for its abhorrent treatment of Okie migrants. White, brown, black, red, yellow—sure, color matters here, but not as much as money. If you're poor you're disposable. And invisible. Which are one and the same around these parts. It's why Steinbeck tossed his journalist's steno and decided fiction was the only way to get at the whole truth. In his diary, he scribbled: *I want to put a tag of shame on the greedy bastards who are responsible for this.* Twenty years later Visalia gets another nod in Capote's *In Cold Blood,* as the town where the slain Bonnie Clutter's brother lives. Visalia has its own literary legacy but works hard to deny it. Books here are the devil's doing. Which is why it was among the first counties to ban and burn Steinbeck's tale of Tom Joad swearing vengeance against the dogs of big agriculture. Here, the legacy of erasure gets passed from generation to generation like an heirloom. This is why even today it is a city of 300,000 eyeballs and not a single bookstore. Independent thinking is overshadowed by the gospel of megachurches, where John Deere is the preacher, and there's enough crushed grapes flowing to keep everybody numb. Its legacy persists. You just have to look beneath the manure and the blossoms to find it. When I hear the name Visalia, I pay attention.

The woman sees me glancing over my shoulder. After the third time she asks if we know one another. I tell her no, but that I couldn't help overhear her mention Visalia.

"Are you from Visalia?" she asks. I nod. And this is how our conversation begins. She asks what I do for a living. I tell her I'm a writer.

"Have you written anything I might've heard of?"

Out of respect for the other passengers, I lean in and whisper, "I wrote a book about a plane crash that happened in 1948."

"Wait. Are you the guy I heard about on the news who's been searching for families?"

"Yes, that's me."

"That's incredible. How many passengers have you found so far?"

"Seven," I say. "So far."

"Ain't that something," she says, while glancing at the other passengers.

We talk. When I mention "braceros" her eyes open.

"I have a coworker you should speak with," she says. "I believe he recorded his father-in-law on video talking about his days as a bracero. I can put you in touch with him if you'd like."

This type of invitation has become common over the last few years. Someone always knows someone who was once a bracero, and always they want me to speak with them. Early on I was reluctant to take up these offers. I didn't want to be pigeonholed as the guy who writes about braceros. This wasn't my interest. It still isn't. I am specifically after the people's stories. The anecdotes that make them human. That they were brought to the United States by way of a guest worker program was a peripheral circumstance to me. But time has taught me much. I've since adopted a more open attitude about it all. I've learned that the stories I'm after aren't necessarily the ones that are after me. So this woman, whose name I learn is Kelly, offers to put me in touch with her friend Peter. I give her my information. Chances are nothing will come of it. Chances are I am wrong.

5

THE SOLE SURVIVOR

IT IS THE YEAR 2008 when Peter Cannon, a Visalia middle-school teacher, decides he will interview his father-in-law, who had been a bracero during World War II. An amateur videographer, Peter captures the interview on tape. His father-in-law's name is Salvador Yeo Rodríguez. Salvador was twenty-one years old when the plane crash at Los Gatos Canyon happened, and his memory of the incident is still intact, sixty years after that fateful day. When the old man is prompted by his son-in-law, he recalls the details with great clarity. It's important to remember that at the time this video is being recorded there's been no mention of the plane crash in any newspapers or television broadcasts, and social media isn't a factor because it's still nascent. My book *All They Will Call You* will not come out for another nine years. In short, Salvador has no ulterior motive for fabricating the incident of the plane crash. Peter asks his father-in-law a simple question: *Can you tell me about your time as a bracero?*

Salvador is seated just feet away from the camera. His face is dark-complected and gaunt, and his white hair is neatly combed to one side. He wears a blue button-up shirt for the occasion. He stares directly into the camera:

> *They took me to the state of Wisconsin, in Appleton. I worked for a paper factory. They treated us fine there, they were mostly Christians. But there were places where they didn't treat us so good. I remember they took us*

to pick cherries. World War II was still happening. I was in the trees picking, and one day there was a big celebration in the streets, music and dancing, they had announced that the war was over. It was a big fiesta. And, uh . . . in those years . . . well, just like now, they would get people without papers and deport them. And, uh, it happened to me once. They caught me in Stockton, California, and from there they took me to . . . San Pedro [sic]. And from San Pedro the planes took the group of undocumented people. And it happened to me. But there was a plane that left just before me, and it was full of undocumented people, and it took off for Juárez [sic]. That's where some of the planes were going. So, the next plane took off, and that's the one I was on. I wasn't able to get on the first plane because it was too full. But I was in line to get on that first flight. But I didn't fit, so I got on the second plane. So, the first plane that took off . . . it crashed, right before it arrived to Texas [sic] . . . it crashed. Everybody died. But we didn't realize that the other plane had crashed. Until I got to Juárez and they told me that the same guys who were in the waiting room with us at the detention facility . . . they told me, "That plane you were going to board crashed." And some of the guys from the waiting room thought that I had boarded that plane. I almost got on that plane too, but I didn't. [Pause.] That happened . . . in the year . . . 1948.

Sic means there are holes in Salvador's testimony. Of course, these can be attributed to time and memory. But based on his testimony we now know there was a second airplane that morning. Possibly more. Which means there were far more than twenty-eight Mexicanos awaiting deportation that day. A fact that only increases the possibility of their survival. Each passenger had a 50 percent chance of choosing the right airplane, depending on where in line they stood. Salvador was perhaps number 30 or 31 in line, because he admits he "almost got on that plane," but it was "too full."

After viewing Salvador's testimony, I immediately begin searching records and manifests for information as to whether there were more planes that morning, but I'm unsuccessful. Over the course of a few years, I return, again and again, studying the video of Salvador Yeo Rodríguez too many times to count.

What stands out is that his memory of that day has three obvious flaws. He recalls the plane having left "San Pedro," which is in Southern California, despite claiming that he was picked up in Stockton, which is in Northern California, near Sacramento. Stockton is also where several of the other passengers were picked up before being taken to the deportation center in San Francisco, and then later to Oakland, where the plane would depart. Not San Pedro, as Salvador suggests. He also remembers the plane crashing down "before it arrived to Texas," presumably headed to "Juárez," the sister city of El Paso (where I live). However, as we now know, the plane crashed down in California's Central Valley (where I'm from). And this might all be too much of a stretch, except that when he's asked about the date, Salvador reaches back into his memory, takes a split second to recall, and then says, with certainty in his eyes, yes, "This happened in the year 1948."

In the year 1948 there are no reports of any other plane that crashed while carrying Mexican bracero workers. In fact, there are no reports of a plane crash that had been carrying Mexicans at any other time in the history of the United States. This was one specific incident that has happened only one time. What Salvador Yeo Rodríguez is retrieving from his memory is the morning when he survived the fate of the plane crash at Los Gatos Canyon.

6

THE UNEARTHING OF ALBERTO RAIGOZA CARLOS

Mexico City, Colonia Tlalcoligia, July 2019

DOÑA OFELIA MORALES turns her back to me as she hovers over the stove tending to her mole. I've been sitting at her small table, taking in the details of her kitchen, for the last thirty minutes. Moments ago, a hard rain was battering this corrugated part of the city, but now it's gone, and in its place is an awkward silence. I've learned that there's much to discover in the silence if you sit with it. But it wasn't always this way. Talking with strangers has never come easy to me. Especially when the environment is unfamiliar. As a kid I was painfully shy, and in Spanish even more so. I still am. But I've learned to befriend silence. Also, it's clear that doña Ofelia is intent on cooking up a feast, and I don't want to interrupt her flow with my questions. So I wait patiently under the close watch of her daughters and grandchildren. Outside, her pack of Chihuahua dogs snarl at anyone who strolls past this part of Tlalcoligia, a cluttered neighborhood at the southern heel of the city. Her home is typical in these parts. A brightly painted cinderblock construct attached to a labyrinth of endless houses, speckled with vines and varieties of cacti poking out from cracks in the concrete. Her kitchen is the central space of the house. Next to it, a separate space that functions as both bedroom and living room. Outside, a cement patio deck with a sink and faucet for washing the dishes.

Doña Ofelia turns to me, her head engulfed in a ribbon of steam. "Espero que hayas venido con hambre," she says. I assure her that I'm very hungry.

"Huele muy rico," I reply. Her grandchildren smile at me. It's the first time they hear me put more than two words together in Spanish.

I help her daughters Maria, Ivonne, and Xóchitl carry the table and chairs to the patio outside, where we'll have our meal. Her granddaughters spread a floral cloth across the table. They carry out bowls of salsa and place them in the center. I try helping but they swat me away from the kitchen. "You just sit down," Maria instructs me. I try again, but my effort is met with a wicked side-eye, so I do as ordered.

൭

Locating Alberto Raigoza Carlos makes this the ninth passenger of the plane crash that I have found so far. In the only photo of "Betito" that exists, he's eighteen years old, just two years shy of meeting his fate. He's holding a child—a little girl, dressed humbly, with a white bib, white shoes with floppy laces, both ears pierced, dark hair, and wide eyes. Betito's face is youthful, with the eyes of a boy, goofy and innocent, but curious. He wears a dinner jacket, perhaps one size too small, and his jet-black hair is curly and slightly unkempt. His earlobes are long, and his right hand, with which he braces the child, is immense for his age. The child stares slightly above the camera's lens, at whoever is standing behind it. It's clear she's content in her uncle's arms. The child is Ofelia Morales, age one. Alberto is her only uncle. Her mother is Carlota Raigoza, affectionately referred to as Mamá Carlota, Alberto's sister and only blood sibling. This is how Maria, Ofelia's youngest daughter, has explained it to me.

Maria contacted me in early 2018, after she'd been looking for information on her family. She found an online article with my name and email on it. She told me that she lived in Utah, but that her mother was still in Mexico City. Following a year of phone conversations, I informed Maria that I'd be in Mexico City that summer, and she agreed to meet me at her mother's house. She said she had flying points with an airline and was due home for a visit. This is when she first told me about her occupation. Of all the jobs Maria could've had, she happened to work for a major airline company.

Alberto Raigoza Carlos with baby Ofelia, circa 1946.

Maria helps her mother ladle the mole onto plates. The girls bring out a pitcher of blood-red hibiscus and serve me a glass with ice. I try helping them fill the glasses, but they're also skilled in the art of the side-eye, so I'm forced back into my seat. They laugh. I wait patiently as dish after dish is brought to the table: mole de pollo, arroz, tortillas, salsa, it's bliss. Everyone takes a seat and waits until doña Ofelia finally sits down. And just as she does, her dogs bark at the gate.

"Elvira ya llegó," she says. She gets back up from her chair and goes to open it.

Maria whispers to me, "Elvira knew Alberto, they were good friends."

Her sister Xóchitl brings two more chairs to the table. Doña Ofelia introduces us.

Doña Elvira Perjuán is a petite woman, barely four feet tall, and speaks in a low whisper. She knows exactly why I'm there, and as she sits down she starts right in.

Doña Elvira Perjuán: "I am ninety-five years old. When Betito died I was just twenty-four. It was very difficult for me. He and I were good friends . . . best friends. He taught me so much. He's the one who taught me how to read and write. He was an artist, you know, he knew how to make paintings on wood, metal, on anything he could find. He also knew how to embroider. Yes, he did . . . he embroidered. And he's the one who taught me. It's not common for men to know how to embroider. But he knew how to do those things, and he taught me. We used to read together, and paint together. And, well, I loved him very much. Some people say that he and I were supposed to be together. Some say that. [*Pause.*] I really liked him. And he liked me. But we were just very good friends, yes."

There's a gleam in her eye. Doña Ofelia serves her a plate of mole, and doña Elvira takes in the aroma. She grasps doña Ofelia's hands, approvingly. And in that small exchange, what I see are two young women, bonded by the closeness of their past. We eat and breathe together, and sit quietly in the presence of these two matriarchs. Doña Ofelia picks up where she left off—

The story goes that when her grandmother Antonia Carlos was giving birth to her uncle Betito, there were complications that required Antonia to make the kind of decision no mother should ever be faced with—it was either the baby's life or her own. Both would not survive. No one recalls what the issues were, just that fate had dealt the family this blow from the very beginning. Antonia opted to spare the baby. She gave birth to Betito, and moments later drew her last breath. She never got to hold him. Not once. She could only look up at the glistening face of her baby boy, long enough to smile, before drifting off to the realm of the ancestors.

But there's another version of this story. The one on *official* record. According to the 1930 Mexican census, Antonia did get to hold Betito. Not only did she survive the birth, but she lived long enough to see him turn two, and her daughter Carla turn eight. The record claims they lived in San Juan Bautista de Teúl, Zacatecas.

When I mention this to doña Ofelia she lifts a forkful of mole to her lips and ponders it a moment. She tilts her head and stares at me; her eyes do not blink. "That paper's wrong. My grandmother died giving birth to Betito. Everyone knows this." And of course, she's right. How else to justify the weight of grief she's inherited? As if it wasn't bad enough that Betito would be killed in a plane crash and his whereabouts unknown, the fact that his own mother sacrificed her life just so that he could survive is what laced the story with its cursed overtone. One way or another, Betito just wasn't meant to live. This is the lore doña Ofelia was raised on, and paper be damned, it shaped the person she is today.

Antonia's untimely death meant that José Cruz, Betito's father, was now left alone with both children to care for. In those times it was a common understanding, as it was with my own grandfather, that no man alone was equipped to raise children, especially if one child happened to be a girl, and José Cruz was no exception. His options, as far as he was concerned, were to either find a woman willing to mother the children, or give them up for adoption. Though not without a long period of consideration, José Cruz decided to give them up. Besides, it was his good friend, El Licensiado Miguel Mora, and his humble wife Sarita whom the children would go to. And that the couple had children of their own made it an ideal fit. So, at around ages two and eight, Betito and Carlota went to live with the Mora family in Mexico City. A father faced with a choice about raising his children, a son and daughter—the parallel to my own life is not lost on me. But that isn't the story I'm here to explore. I came to learn about Betito.

The family quietly contemplates the events, as forks scrape against plates. I remain in my head. Until this moment I had never been to Mexico City. Though I am new here, it doesn't feel foreign to me. None of this does.

Earlier this morning I took a walk around the neighborhood, processing all that this latest trek to Mexico had put in my path. I strolled along the broken streets that rose and fell around every turn. Old buildings, and the smell of raw meat emanating from butcher blocks. Hunks of ice melting in buckets, and staticky music spewing from tiny radios. Every inch of the city pulsed and felt intimate to me. Not in some fetishized Jack Kerouac fellaheen Mexico City way, but in the most motherly tongue I could hear the city speaking to me, whispering clues. I took photos and recorded audio of the streets, not as a tourist but as a lost son. Not knowing if or when I would return again. It's in these strolls, these breaks, that I revisit my purpose. Why I am here, listening to these stories. I can't help but think about our own Betito, my mom's baby brother. And how we never found him. Is it possible I'm applying the voices of people like doña Ofelia and doña Elvira to my own family? Had my grandparents remained alive long enough to offer me their own consejos, what might they say about my search? Perhaps the words of these matriarchs fit my wounds. With each interview, and each conversation, a subtle cauterization is at work. A gentle process of tiny closures. With each wrinkled gaze, and each serving of a warm meal, I hear my grandparents' disembodied voices: "It's okay, mijo, you're doing your best . . . you'll find what you're looking for." I am convinced our histories are two embers of one flame that is fast being extinguished. And the people who keep it, these Storykeepers, faster yet. This is why I treat each visit as if it's the one and only chance I have. Because sometimes it is.

Maria breaks the silence: "Mamá Sara was a nice woman, her and El Licensiado were both very kind people. They loved Mamá Carlota and my tío Betito. But Mamá Carlota was already older by then, and really independent. And from what I was told, a hard young woman too, she didn't let anyone boss her around. She even had tattoos!" Everyone laughs. The mood lifts. "She had a big tattoo on her arm. It was a giant ship," her sister Ivonne concurs.

"Did you ever ask her why she had a giant ship on her arm?"

"Yes, but all she said was . . . well, you do stupid things for love." Doña Ofelia smiles.

"Did she ever tell you that story?"

"She would say things sometimes, yes." Maria hesitates.

Ivonne cuts in. "Mamá Carlota had a very, um, how would you say it, adventurous story—"

7

MAMÁ CARLOTA'S STORY

When Carlota turned sixteen, she made an important decision for herself—it was time to leave the Mora household. The only issue was that she and Betito were as close as any two siblings can be, and at just ten years old he was still too young to go with her. So she made her little brother a promise. When she turned eighteen, she would return for him, and they would live together until the end of their days. It was a promise that Betito held on to. The Moras had raised their children to believe in the power of Diosito. They taught them prayers and recited them nightly. A practice the children leaned heavily on.

For the most part, life with the Mora family was stable. Filled with routine, work, perhaps schooling, as El Licensiado was an educated man and took pride in making sure the children were regarded as such. It was during this time that Betito would discover that he was an artist. He began painting wooden plates and bowls for the tourists, making toys out of clay, and eventually learning to embroider. "It was a simple but good life," doña Ofelia recalls, lifting a scoop of mole to her lips.

And just as promised, on the morning of her eighteenth birthday Carlota arrived on horseback, on the steps of the Moras' house, there to retrieve her little brother. Her hair was cropped short and she wore the outfit of a revolutionary, including a rifle. She climbed down from the horse, went inside, and kindly greeted the Moras. Mamá Sara embraced Carlota and didn't try and convince her otherwise. Betito, now twelve, heard his sister's voice and rushed out to see. They lunged for one another and held on for several minutes. After which Carlota ordered him to get his belongings. It was time. There was nothing Mamá Sara could say or do. And El Licensiado, being a pragmatic man, knew it was probably for the best. It's likely he would've offered them a little money, but one could just as likely see Carlota respectfully declining.

"You've done enough for my brother and me, we won't require any more of your hospitality. Thank you." With that, the two siblings climbed atop the horse and bade the Moras goodbye. El Licensiado and Mamá Sara watched as Carlota and Betito rode away on horseback, two kids practically, away from their lives once and for all, and out into the gamble of wilder Mexico.

In their rememberings are their truths. I'm reminded of this quote by the oral historian Studs Terkel. It isn't my job to question the veracity of their story. It's only my job to document.

"Mamá Carlota would tell us these stories. I don't know if they were true or not, but this was what she told us." There's more—

Later that night, Carlota and Betito met up with a small band of guerrilleros who smuggled guns for the revolutionaries. It's possible this was an offshoot of the Feminine Brigade of Saint Joan of Arc, a lingering faction of the Cristero War, prominent around Mexico City in those years, though no one really knows for sure. Only that Carlota now "looked like a man" and carried guns and collected tattoos. Carlota assured Betito that this was only temporary. "Just long enough to save money. Then we'll find a ranch of our own and live there, with our own horses and no one to bother us."

It was a dream that Betito clutched tightly, and he pitched in any chance he got. By the time he was sixteen he was already skilled in the ways of handling guns, horses, harvests, embroidery, paintbrushes, and just about any task that was put in his way.

But as the saying goes, *Uno pone y Dios dispone.* And isn't that the painful truth? Plan as we might, God laughs and undoes the plan.

Carlota couldn't predict that she'd fall head over bootheels for a man. Not just any man, but one so experienced in life, so resourceful and knowledgeable, that she found it a relief to finally have an equal. His name was Daniel Morales, and he was a free diver from Acapulco. It was rumored that with just one gulp of air he could touch the ocean's floor and sing all the verses of "En mi viejo San Juan" on his way up—a near-supernatural feat that made him a legend in his hometown. How the two crossed paths no one knows, and Mamá Carlota never offered. The only thing that was certain was that once they had come into each other's lives they were inseparable. Betito took to Daniel like a brother, and the three were instantly a family. They planned their life together, and things were set in motion.

By now the United States was in the middle of World War II, and bracero recruiting stations were spreading throughout central Mexico, and young men were heading to el Norte by the trainload. Daniel had come and gone a couple of times, and he knew very well that there was money to be made. Betito, now seventeen years old, a man by all standards, was ready to head north, to provide for his family and hopefully manifest their lofty but tangible dream. It took little convincing for Carlota to be on board, as she too could see that an opportunity like this would only benefit them all.

Doña Ofelia gets up from her chair and disappears into the bedroom. Maria continues telling me the story: "I'm sure Mamá Carlota felt safe knowing that Betito was going with Daniel, so they could watch out for each other. Betito was still young when he started working as a bracero, but he and Daniel were very close, so it made sense that they went together."

Doña Elvira lifts the photo of Alberto up, stares at it a moment, then kisses it. She squints and looks again. Her eyes tear up. She glances at me. No words come to her. She looks back at the photo. She stares and stares. As if the longer she stares the farther back in time she is transported.

Doña Ofelia returns clutching a tin cookie container.

"My mom has a surprise for you," Maria says. She opens the container and lifts out a few old letters. She takes one of the envelopes, peeks into it. The energy shifts. Doña Ofelia offers me the envelope. As with all ephemera, from the moment my fingertips touch it I pay attention to the vibrational pull. I lift it to my nose, smell it. Press it to my chest, hold it there a few seconds. No one finds this strange. They know exactly what I'm doing and why.

Doña Ofelia tells me, "This is the last letter Betito wrote home to Carlota, mi mamá." She hesitates. "Go ahead, read it—"

While living in Colorado, I shared an office with a graphologist. She taught me that there's a lot you can learn about a person by looking deeply into a letter, beyond the message. The paper it's written on, for instance, or the way it's folded, even the ink. The subtle shifts in lettering. There are stains at the top of Alberto's letter, which could be grease stains, or oils from fingers, or food. They could've been from Alberto, or they could've been from the hands of his sister Carlota after receiving it. And when he writes the address at the top left-hand corner, it's the only time he doesn't use cursive. It's block lettering. He wants his location to be absolutely clear. And from the lean of his letters, slightly to the right, we can tell that he's mature for his age, emotionally stable. His *t*s are open, but not too open, as he's still slightly reserved but youthful. We know this because of the playfulness in the sweeping *S* and *C* and *R* in his sister's name. The paper is not lined, yet his sentences are fairly straight, so it's also fair to assume Alberto is a disciplined young man. Curiously, there are water stains that appear on the words:

year 48
Daniel
come for
know
lives

It's possible, and likely, that these are teardrops. If it were sweat his hands and wrists would've likely smeared other parts of the writing, but they did not. The droplets seem to have fallen directly onto the letter, from above. As for what Alberto wants us to know, the letter is dated just three weeks before the plane crash, and he's writing to us from a boarding house in the coastal town of Salinas, California. Two hours from where I grew up. According to the return address on the envelope, the exact location he's at in this moment is 71 Monterey Road. Months later I'll find the building, and it'll still be there, a small rectangular unit adjacent to the train tracks. He sits down to compose this letter. He's alone, which is to say his brother-in-law Daniel is not with him. Not in this moment. How he ended up alone no one knows. But it wasn't supposed to be that way. And this is the reason he's writing home to Carlota.

1 - 3 – 48

Sra: Carlota Raigoza Carlos

Querida hermana, in this time I am sending you my hellos and hoping you are doing well, and that you're in perfect health, a Dios gracias! First of all, please receive a thousand hugs and kisses for yourself, for my little Ofelia, and for Daniel, and also, may it be one happy and prosperous New Year 1948! I received Daniel's letter, in which he says that he'll be coming back here either at the end of this month, or in February, but it makes me happy to know you two are together and can see each other at this time. . . .

. . . please ask Daniel to tell me if he's coming back to Salinas, because in his letter he wasn't clear, or I didn't understand if he meant they weren't going to send any more braceros, so please tell him to write me as soon as possible, letting me know if he's coming or not . . . and with this, kisses to Ofelia and to you a thousand hugs and kisses, and for Daniel lots of hugs, and please tell him to write to me.

Alberto Raigoza

A Raigoza G.
71 Monterey R.D.
Salinas Calif.

Salinas Calif - 1 - 3 - 48

Sra: Carlota Raigoza Cobo

Querida hermana en la precente los saludo y espero
Estén bien que yo asta la precente en perfecta salud
a Dios gracias:
Pues pofo ante todo te digo que resibas un millón
de abrazos y besos para ti y para mi Ofelia y Daniel
y despues un feliz y prospero año 48 y luego te
digo que recibí una carta de Daniel en la que me
dise que al fin de este mes viene por aca o para
febrero pues cuanto me agradaría que fuera cierto
Que felicidad estar los dos juntos viendo uno por el
otro
Saber Que te mande un paquete con 5 cortes para vestido
y 2 cortes para traje para mi pero no se si pazarán porque
Margarita la esposa del mayordomo fue al correo aqui en
Salinas y le dijeron que no sabian si pazaban ho no
y ella me dijo que los hiba a mandar a una amiga
a nogales arizona y que ella vive en nogales Sonora
y que pudiera ser que asi pazarán asi que estate
al pendiente si llega ese bulto de nogales
ese es y dile a Daniel que me diga bien como
es que se ba a benir porque en su carta no entiendo
aqui se sabe que no ban a venir mas brazeros

Page 1 of Alberto's letter to Carlota, January 3, 1948.

Perhaps Alberto remained at the same boarding house for three more weeks, waiting to receive a response from Daniel, hoping he would return. Or perhaps the boarding house is where he was picked up by the Immigration and Naturalization Service. Doña Ofelia doesn't recall Mamá Carlota ever saying. We only know that twenty-five days after writing this letter, Alberto "Betito" Raigoza Carlos, age twenty, baby brother to Carlota, brother-in-law to Daniel Morales, and uncle to little Ofelia Morales, was made to board a Douglas DC-3 airplane in Oakland, California, on the morning of January 28, 1948, and by 10:38 a.m. Pacific time, he was in the middle of a nightmare that he would not wake up from. It was a flight he was never meant to survive.

. . . *may it be one happy and prosperous New Year 1948!*

Betito's final words echo.

I look up from the letter. Doña Elvira is rocking slightly. She has a heavy but distant gaze, Alberto's photo clutched to her chest. The family knows what I have just read. They've committed the letter to memory.

Doña Ofelia lifts another letter out of the cookie tin.

"Here's one more I think you should read," she says, handing it to me. Even the dogs are quiet now. I open it. This letter is from Mamá Sara to Carlota, written just six days after the accident.

February 3, 1948

Señora Carlota R. de Morales,

Mi muy querida Carlota. This Sunday I found out through the newspaper the misfortune that happened to Alberto, but I didn't want to write to you because I wasn't sure yet if it was him. But then I learned that it was the same Alberto that we all know and love, and since that day I haven't forgotten about you. I can only imagine how bad you must feel, you who loved him dearly and did so much for him, and he was your only brother, that's why you must feel inconsolable, but that is the will of God, and we have no choice but to abide by what he has done. Please say all the prayers you can for the eternal rest of his soul, and let us hope for the day that God has him in his glory. I give you my heart, and condolences, and send our hello to Daniel, don Chicho, and to Ofelia many kisses. And for you, please receive my embraces.

Mamá Sara

It was through the local newspaper that the family heard of Alberto's death. And we know it spread as far as Uruapan, Michoacán, because Carlota also received a letter from her comadre Dolores, written the same day as Mamá Sara's letter, February 3. She writes: *Alberto was a good kid, loved in all parts of Mexico, and he will be very missed. . . .*

I glance at the faces of Alberto's descendants. They stare back at me. They have held on to this grief for more than seventy years. In this moment I forget what exactly I have come searching for. A "book" seems like a shallow purpose when faced with real human lives staring back at you, as if you might be able to answer *why* things had to be this way. *Why* did Betito have to die in such an undignified manner? *Why* was his body tossed into a mass grave so far from home? *Why* no headstone? No name? They want answers, and they deserve them. But I have none. And the ones accountable for those decisions have long since passed. I wonder what it will take for this family to find closure. One thing is true for all of us: when we die, we expect, at the very least, to retain our dignity. Dignity, from the Latin *dignus*—worthiness. We are born worthy. Our names are the most basic part of that worthiness. They prove our connections and our existence. And we are worthy of honoring these connections, evidence that our lives once meant something to someone, that we were a part of something greater than us. We were, and are, kin to the living. Don't we deserve to have that recognized? Our name on a headstone is the most ancient of ways to exhibit this. Our obituary in a newspaper, maybe even our photo, are others. We are worthy of at least this much. And for the ones who survive us, it's about closure. A necessary step if they hope to one day find comfort in the high notes of our lives. But to get there they must first walk down the corridor of letting go. And to let go, steps must be taken. Rituals must be performed. Grief must be confronted. Isn't this why my mother took me to find her baby brother Betito's grave when I was just a boy? To witness again what took place? To be certain it did happen, and to feel validated for the grief she's held all these years? To pass it back through the heart?

Ivonne speaks up: "Mamá Carlota practically raised me and my sisters. We stayed with her a lot and she would tell us these stories. She spoke about Betito all the time. She always kept an altar for him, she believed in God."

Maria: "Yes, that's true. She would make us pray with her all the time too. She would actually take us to the rooftop, that's where she liked to pray. She said she was closer to God that way. And when we were just kids, well, we didn't question that. We just went up to the rooftop with her, at night, under the stars. And she would take her rosary out and make us pray with her. And those prayers were always for her baby brother, Betito." She pauses. "I wish she had lived long enough to meet you."

Me with Betito's family, Mexico City, 2019.

8

A BEGINNING

I told Bea I was leaving. She had been thinking about it all night and was resigned to it. . . . We turned at a dozen paces, for love is a duel, and looked at each other for the last time.

—JACK KEROUAC, *ON THE ROAD: THE ORIGINAL SCROLL*

ര

August 30, 2013

IT'S FRIDAY MORNING, and I'm at Belmont Memorial Cemetery in Fresno, at the graveside of a woman named Bea Franco. National Public Radio is here, and so is the *L.A. Times*. They report: *Bea Franco, the real woman behind Terry the Mexican Girl of Jack Kerouac's famous novel* On the Road, *has died at age 92*. She's the subject of the book I've just written, *Mañana Means Heaven*. In the past six decades since *On the Road* was first published, she'd been marginally written about in over twenty books, yet no one had ever actually looked for her. Her "story" was authored without her knowing it. In 2008, I began searching for her family, only to discover that Bea herself was still alive and lived a mile down my street. With her permission and involvement, I wrote the book based on her true-life story. But the synchronicities have only just begun. Her family is gathered. The father sprinkles holy water and recites a prayer. Albert, her son, asks me to say a few words. The hum of traffic from Highway 99 is intrusive, so I keep it short. "Bea's life is a testament to the power of our individual stories. I was lucky to have met her . . ." I hear people whisper, "This story was lost to history. She was lost to history." My daughter Rumi, nine years old, tugs at my elbow, "Daddy, doesn't your book come out today?" She's right. I was so troubled by Bea's passing that I forgot today is the official release date. "You're right," I say. On the very day we are lowering Bea's body into the earth, her story takes flight.

September 2, 2013

Just three days after Bea's funeral, I'm at Holy Cross Cemetery, on the other side of Highway 99, a stone's throw from where we buried Bea. We are unveiling the memorial headstone for the thirty-two victims of the plane crash at Los Gatos. We've spent months raising funds to make this happen, and now it's here. Eight hundred people attend, including the family members of the victims I've found to date. They include the Ramírez family, the family of pilot Frank Atkinson, and the family of Martin Hoffman, the musician who composed the melody to the song. Priests sprinkle holy water and words are spoken. I'm staring down at the names on the headstone, and I'm thinking of Bea Franco. It was the search for her that led me to the plane crash, which then led me to the names. Both stories bound by an invisible thread. All the major news outlets are here. Cameras everywhere. It's both a celebration and a funeral. Tears are shed. Grief and joy are one. I'm asked to say a few words: "This headstone is a testament to the power of our names. We're lucky to have some of the families here with us . . ." People whisper, "This story was lost to history. These people were lost to history." I see the names on the headstone. They symbolize lives. But what of the lives? Who are they? Who survives them? And why do I find myself here now, standing between two burial grounds, enveloped by the past?

9

EARLY LESSONS IN INVESTIGATION

Jack Kerouac Archives, New York Public Library, June 2009

I'M HERE TO SEE one thing and one thing only: the letters that Bea Franco wrote to Jack in late 1947. I'm granted access, and I spend the better part of a day with Bea's letters in my hands, finding clues about who she was. I learn she is close to her brother Alex. I learn she has an address in Selma, California, where she picked grapes. I learn that her middle initial is R. With each detail I learn I feel myself drawing closer to her. I take notes. I whisper into my handheld recorder. I can feel the archivist observing me. Or maybe he doesn't. It's possible I'm just paranoid. Years of conditioning have convinced me that I am an impostor in these spaces. I can't ignore the distrust settling in my stomach. There are questions brewing inside me. I want to ask them, but I'm intimidated by all the stuffy, unfriendly faces in the room. But then it hits me. These are strangers, and I'm sure they don't even notice me here, a brown man, in the Kerouac archives. I could be one of Ralph Ellison's ghosts. I convince myself. And since they don't *see* me, and since I don't belong here, I'm free to say pretty much anything. I'm emboldened. I wave the archivist over. "How can I get permission to publish Bea Franco's letters?" He replies, "You would need permission from her family." But when I ask him for the family's contact he tells me it doesn't exist. In fact, he chuckles. "No one's ever found her or her family," he says. "They're probably in Mexico, who knows?" It's more than likely that this attitude is why no one has ever bothered looking for Bea. He walks away. It doesn't sit well with me. When he circles back, I press him: "How did other biographers get permission to publish excerpts of her letters in *their* books?" He hesitates, "Well, if you can prove that you've made attempts to locate her family then we'll have you sign a hold harmless form. You can publish her letters that way. But then you'd be liable if the family ever does come forth and claims you didn't have permission." It's all I need to hear.

I fly back to California, and the next day I drive to Selma, the last residence Bea wrote on her letters. I have no idea where to start. I know nothing about investigation, aside from what I've seen on television or read in books. But there's something dormant inside of me. A gravity I can't deny. Something about searching just makes sense to me. I park at a gas station that still has a telephone booth. I grab the yellow pages and look up the last name Franco. I'm naïve in my methods, but I'm aware of this, and so protocols don't apply to me. There are only a handful of Francos in Selma, according to the page. I tear it from the phone book and call each one then and there. I start at the top of the list and work my way down. With just a few questions I can weed out some of the families. Some hang up on me. I call them right back. I'm relentless. I take notes, jot down names, and investigate every lead I have. I'm convinced she's dead by now. I call cemeteries asking if "Bea R. Franco" is buried there. They ask me what the "R" stands for and I tell them I don't know. I spend three afternoons walking up and down every cemetery I can find, scanning headstones. Like this I go through the last half of 2009 searching for Bea and her family. I'm about to give up. But before I do, I try one more approach. I go back to the yellow pages and look up private investigators. I run my finger over each of their names. None feel right. But then I find one who advertises that she has an English degree. Jackpot. An investigator who appreciates a good story.

I call Adrianne Allen and tell her Bea's story. She's hooked. But then I tell her I only have a budget of one hundred dollars and sheepishly ask how much investigation that buys me. She laughs outright. And then a long silence. "I'll help you," she finally says. Our agreement is this: She'll look up information and tell me where to go and what to ask for. But the legwork, knocking on doors and making calls, is mine to do. We have a deal. I don't know this in the moment, but this arrangement will become my crash course in audacity, the most invaluable lesson. It will be the best hundred dollars I've ever spent. Her instructions are simple and direct. She tells me, "Go to the Fresno County Hall of Records, start there. Say you're related to Bea if you have to, see what they have. And keep asking questions until they let you in. And always go in person when you can. It'll get you farther than a phone call or email." I trust her experience and do as she says. This emboldens me to enter again those spaces where I don't belong—government offices, stuffy administration rooms, newspaper archive departments. Day by day my courage grows. I ask questions, begin to walk as if I belong there. Adrianne reminds me, "Act first, apologize later." This advice is a game changer. At the hall of records I tug open drawers, stick my nose into a pile of death certificates. Act like I belong there. Start believing I do. At the Old Selma Winery a *No Trespassing* sign hangs on a fence. I enter through the back. Sign? What sign? The world opens up to me. I feel unstoppable.

But after a few months neither Adrianne nor I have located any of Bea's relatives. My hundred dollars runs out, and she helps me for another two weeks. Finally, when it seems we've exhausted every last possibility she sends me a receipt, generously listing only half the work, showing I have paid in full. I call her one last time to thank her for everything. She wishes me good luck and offers a parting word of advice. It's in the form of a question.

"Have you ever considered that Bea might still be alive?"

"What makes you say that?"

"In my experience, dead people are easier to find than living people. Dead people leave a trail: lots of records, obituaries, stuff like that. It's very possible Bea's still alive."

Up until that very moment, I had honestly never considered the real probability that Bea Franco could actually be alive.

10

TRANSFERENCE

IN THE MONTHS AFTER Bea's funeral, I would spend a series of nights in her room, sleeping on her old bed, with her clothes still hanging in the doorless closet. Much like my grandmother Estela Constante, Bea too was a collector of sentimental things. Her room was cluttered with statuettes and knickknacks she'd kept over decades. Mother's Day cards still hung on her vanity mirror. Doilies on her dresser. Costume jewelry splayed out. Endless shoes and purses clustered in the corners. A bedside lamp of Charlie Chaplin, one of my personal heroes. Her pillowcase and sheets still carried that distinct human smell, a diaphanous layer of lost skin cells and hair embedded in the threads she once rested and dreamed on. Albert was in charge of her belongings and still hadn't found the motivation to remove any of it.

By this time I was living in Colorado but would return to Fresno often to conduct research on the plane crash, so Al would invite me to stay at Bea's house. Sometimes he would be there, but sometimes it was just me. As for the sleeping arrangements, my options were either his mom's room or the couch. It was a no-brainer.

Lying in Bea's bed, I would pull the sheets up over me, lie flat on my back, and absorb what residue of her essence still loomed. Tucked just inches beneath where my heart rested was where she kept her memories:

photos stuffed in shoeboxes, letters and postcards. I slept directly above them, always with an intuitive sense that they would transfer their energy into my subconscious. There were so many things I wanted to ask her but never got the chance to. So much about her life was a mystery. And she preferred it that way.

In her final years, Bea and I had become close. I would visit her often, and we'd talk for hours. On her ninetieth birthday we drank scotch and smoked cigarettes from midday to sunset. Sometimes we would talk by phone, and she'd ask about the progress. "It's almost done," I assured her, "soon." I was writing with urgency, as she was growing weaker with each passing season. I wanted her to at least live long enough to see her own book in print. This became my goal, and the push I needed to finish.

When the advance copies of *Mañana Means Heaven* finally came out, I pulled the first book from the box and rushed straight to the post office and sent it to her via priority mail. It arrived at her house on August 7, 2013. Bea's daughter, Patricia, took a photo of her holding the book in her hands, smiling. "My mom loves the photo you used for the cover," she texted.

Seven days later Bea was gone. The photo Patricia took that day would turn out to be the only one in existence of Bea holding the book about *her* life in her hands. The only book ever written with her permission, and with her involvement.

To call her a friend is inaccurate. She was more of a guide, in life and perhaps even more so in death. I knew she had come to me for a reason, and it was my job to figure out what that reason was. It was never just her story I was after. There was a larger purpose. It was Bea who shepherded me to the story of the plane crash at Los Gatos. She was the first clue, and the initial portal into that particular past. It seemed every time I typed the name Bea Franco into the search engine, fragments of information about a 1948 plane crash would find me. It was while searching for the labor camp that she and Kerouac stayed at that I first came across the headline: *100 People See Plane Crash to Earth, Farm Labor Disaster.*

Now that *Mañana Means Heaven* was out in the world I had no desire to write another book set in the 1940s. But the plane crash kept pursuing me. *They* kept pursuing me. Eventually I began keeping a file on it, if for no other reason than to appease the ghosts.

I would return every few months, back to Fresno to meet with Al, and each time, after spending a night in Bea's bed, I would leave with the nagging sense that she had unfinished business. She'd always been mysterious during our conversations, but I couldn't tell if she was intentionally leaving out details or if she genuinely didn't remember. Her early years had been rough, so I chalked it up to those blips of memory, those blotches in your past that you experience when you've lived long enough, and especially hard enough. Still, a part of me felt that Bea was protecting herself from something or someone. I felt this strongly, and it kept me paying careful attention, less to the words that came from her mouth and more to the long silences. Those moments when she'd lower her eyes to the floor, or to her coffee mug, as if she didn't hear my question. Sometimes lasting several minutes. Sometimes the silences alone became the conversation. I would listen closely to what she was *not* saying. Over time, it became increasingly clear that whatever she was holding on to she was never going to share with me, or with anyone. And it was best I let it go.

૭

By late fall of 2014, Al told me he was finally going to get rid of his mother's belongings and sell her house. He wanted to know if I'd come over and help him go through all the stuff in her basement in case there was anything of value that the family should keep, by which he meant, in case we found letters between her and Kerouac. I agreed, and we spent the better part of two days donning masks and crawling through the small, musty spaces to dig out boxes of stuff. Just as suspected, we found letters and photos, some dating back to the 1940s, but no correspondence between her and Kerouac. There was, however, a very old bottle of scotch that was unopened and had been kept in the dark for what we estimated was at least forty years. At the end of our search, exhausted and spent, we went inside the house and sat at the dining table. The same spot where I had sat for three years in conversation with Bea. I could still hear her laughter. This moment felt like the end of something, and we both knew it. Al pulled two short glasses from the cupboards, and we opened the scotch. We played some of Bea's old records and drank that entire bottle, sip by sip, sharing stories of his mom. How she'd been through so much but always managed to keep her humor. The stories of her fights and travels. How she ended up being written about and sought after by scholars the world over, all without ever lifting a finger. She was one of those rare muses, so rare that her mere existence merited books and works of art—the kind of anomaly that the universe plants at a certain time and place in history, leaving us with much to contemplate for years to come. But all of that was over now. No more questions, no more recording. Al and I were just two good friends, plain and simple. And it was time to let Bea's memory rest. By now, the plane crash story was calling me.

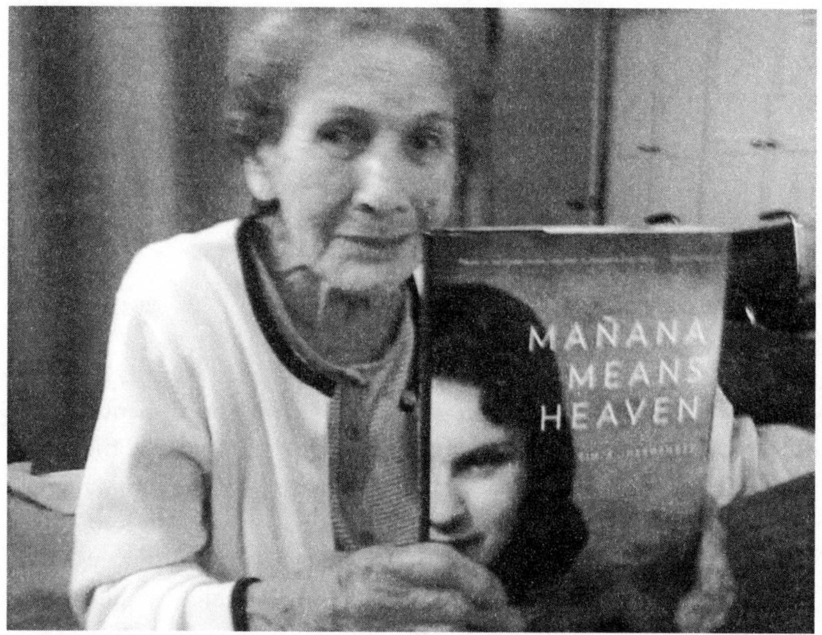

The last photo of Bea Franco, August 2013.

11

VIRGIL

1993

ONE NIGHT, in a drunken blackout, he blows past a stop sign and launches his work truck over a two-hundred-foot bluff on the outskirts of Bakersfield, California. My aunt sees this on the news, and that's how we find out. The reporter mentions they haven't yet found the driver's body. The next day I'm with my mom and her sisters searching for him. We spend the morning investigating the scene for any sign of Virgil. What we find is a disturbing mess. Standing at the edge of the cliff we can see that its slope is at a forty-degree angle, and perhaps this is enough for a person to survive. We hope. But at the very bottom is a wide aqueduct filled with raging water, irrigation for the surrounding agriculture. It's deep. We see no sign of his truck anywhere. We want to believe it's not at the bottom of the aqueduct. The fragmented remains of my uncle's life, his carpenter's tools and clothes, are *scattered like dry leaves* across the incline. I see a single work boot propped against a shrub. I recognize it as his because he's been wearing the same boots since as far back as I can remember. And over there, a few feet away, is his hammer. I know it's his hammer because he and my dad recently helped me build a skateboard ramp in our front yard. Without my realizing it, these images will affect me for years to come. I will know exactly what it looks like to witness one's life in pieces, blown across a mountainside. And I will know the anguish that comes with it.

One by one, carefully, we inch down the cliff, holding on to each other for support, as we comb the terrain looking for clues to Virgil's whereabouts. The whole way down we ask ourselves, and each other, how this could've happened. And of course we all know how it happened. Virgil was drunk. Again. But no one will admit this. Not yet. The entire time my mom and my aunts are silent as they scan the perimeter, trying to keep their emotions in check. I break away from the group, get to work with my own investigations. Farther down the incline I find broken shards of windshield glass. I look closer and see flecks of blood. Virgil's blood. I touch it. Sniff it. I don't want my mom to see, afraid it'll destroy her hopes. It was she, after all, who convinced Virgil that California held a better life for him. It was she who brought him to live here that one summer we found him at that motel in New Mexico. But it's too late. She and her sisters find drops of blood in the dirt. And then a glob. My mother tries not to cry. I can see it in her eyes. In all of their eyes. The trembling, it returns. Witnessing my mom and my aunts huddled together as they search for their baby brother, I can't help but see them as the children of the stories I was raised on. How together, hand in hand, they ran out into the New Mexico night to escape my grandfather's drunken tantrums. Chita, clutching her younger siblings close as they hid behind sagebrush and clusters of cacti, and sometimes in fox dens. First Betito, and now Virgil. Their own ghosts surface in this moment. Mom stares at the aqueduct, and I can see that she's praying her baby brother isn't at the bottom of it. The aqueduct that waters the fields of this part of the San Joaquin Valley. The fields that produce the vegetables and fruits that land on your table. On all our tables. It's quite possible my uncle's blood has made its way to you, and that you've consumed him like holy Eucharist. The evidence is scattered everywhere; pieces of his truck, papers flittering in the breeze, all the particulars of his life decorate the landscape. Everything except Virgil. I slide farther down the incline, and as I get closer to the aqueduct I see more flecks of blood. And then, eventually, small pools of blood. I follow the trail. It seems to stop about halfway down the incline. And then, oddly, the blood moves laterally. Clinging to the incline, I follow it for several yards, until it stops again. It feels like I'm getting closer to something. My heart's racing. I scan the dirt. Unearthing. I lose the trail. A second later, there it is again. A few feet up the incline, more blood. It seems to be ascending. Virgil's blood is now moving back up toward the top of the bluff. I follow it. My mom calls out, "Where're you going?"

"Following the blood," I shout back.

She and my aunts start making their way toward me.

"See?" I point to a purple glob on a rock. They agree he must've climbed out. Yes, we're sure of this now.

We follow the blood until we arrive at the top of the bluff, some fifty yards from where our cars are parked. We calculate that Virgil had to have clawed his way out from the bottom of the cliff. Whether he's alive or not we're unsure. But we agree he's not in the aqueduct. And parts of his body aren't scattered in the dirt, so we know he's intact. Moments later another relative arrives. Her car screeches to a halt. She leaps out, tells us that Virgil came home. "He's at the house right now." What? How? She tells us some high-school kids were out partying last night, and they spotted him, limping and bloody on the side of the road, and took him to get help.

Virgil survived. Of course he did. My aunts are in tears but my mom looks furious. Someone cracks a joke about Virgil being a cat with nine lives. At thirty-six years old he's spent nearly all of them. Most of them while intoxicated. On the drive to see Virgil, I pay attention to my mom's voice, trembling. I can't tell if she's scared or angry. The two sound the same. And because she's scared and angry, without realizing it, so am I. I'm nineteen years old.

This is the third search.

12

A YEAR FOR ANSWERS

There are years that ask questions, and years that answer.
—ZORA NEALE HURSTON, *THEIR EYES WERE WATCHING GOD*

Spring 2019

SIX YEARS have passed since Bea Franco's death. An email appears in my inbox. It's from a woman named Alicia Coronado. She tells me she's read my book *Mañana Means Heaven*, and applauds my accuracy. But then she hits me with an outrageous claim:

Mr. Hernandez, I believe your book is about MY mother.

I know she's wrong. There's no possible way that Bea Franco is her biological mother. I'm wary of people with malign intentions. Besides, it's a known fact that Bea only had two biological children, Albert and his sister Patricia. Both of whom have become like family to me. Bea had never once mentioned a third child. Yet, for some reason, Alicia's claim, as farfetched as it is, intrigues me. I read on.

I was raised in Chowchilla, California, by my biological father and by a woman who I consider my one and only mother, even though she's not my biological mother. Their names are Addy and Jesus. When I was about to go off to college, my parents sat me down and told me this story. They said my biological mother was a woman named Bea Franco, and that she was from Fresno. And that I had two siblings that they knew of . . . I know this sounds crazy, but I was telling my friend about this story and that's when she started Googling my mother's name, and all this stuff popped up. I had no idea. I couldn't believe it. All these articles mentioned your name, so I bought your book, and I read it, and . . . Mr. Hernandez, I believe the book you wrote is about my biological mother, Bea Franco. Everything you say in it describes almost exactly what I was told by my parents . . .

The next day Alicia and I speak by phone. I'm blunt.

"I'm sorry, but I can't just take your word for it. I need proof that you're related."

"That's not possible," she replies, "because my birth certificate doesn't show Bea as my mother. My mom Addy said that my papers were rigged. Keep in mind, this is all based on what my parents told me, but they're both gone now."

"Is there anything you can send me?" I reply.

"My parents did give me one photo. It's of me with Bea."

"You have a photo of you with Bea?"

"Yes, it's the only one my mom kept. I can email it to you right now."

"Please do. And if you don't mind, can you send me a photo of yourself too?"

"Of course, yes, give me a minute, I'll send those right now."

I have no doubt the woman in the photo is Bea Franco. It's taken on the same day as another photo I've seen from her family. Her hair is even styled the same way. In this photo, Bea's kneeling next to a small child, a girl, who is sitting on a scooter. The child is Alicia. Or so Alicia claims. It's compelling. Still, it isn't enough to confirm her story. The next photo is a headshot of Alicia in her younger years. It's a black-and-white, taken when she was in high school. She looks identical to Al, right down to the same hazel eyes and round face. Even to the untrained eye, when they are placed side by side, she and Al are unmistakably related.

"Have you ever seen a photo of Al Franco?" I ask her.

"No, I haven't. Why?"

"Because you two resemble each other."

Silence.

Later that day I phone Al. He tells me that some time ago a woman named Coronado had left a message on his answering machine.

"So you knew about her?"

"The name didn't ring a bell, so I just ignored it."

"She's asking to be put in touch with you."

He's quiet. "That's fine," he says, ambivalent.

"Are you sure?"

"Yeah," he says. "Go ahead."

෴

Months later, Alicia writes to me with an update. She tells me that she's now in frequent contact with Al and Patricia. "I found my siblings," she says. "I'm so glad you wrote that book."

Sometime later I will learn that Alicia was born in September of 1948. If this is her real birthdate then it means she was conceived approximately eight weeks after Bea had her encounter with Jack. As it was told to Alicia by her parents, during the pregnancy Bea left Al and lived with them until the baby was born. After which Bea falsified the birth certificate, and Alicia's life would take a different path than that of her biological siblings. This is the story.

And now it all makes sense.

The reasons Bea evaded my questions about that period of her life. Her long silences. Her distant gaze. Perhaps it was always about a child she had once given up for adoption and kept secret all those years. This was the reason she had been so mysterious. This is why in her responses she tiptoed. Why some things she remembered with great clarity, and others were fuzzy, or else omitted altogether. Never once did she mention a third child. She was protecting herself, and perhaps all three of her children, from the painful choices of her past. "I was stupid when I was younger," she often repeated, whenever I'd ask her about the early days. She'd pause, and then say it again, shaking her head at whatever regret prompted those words.

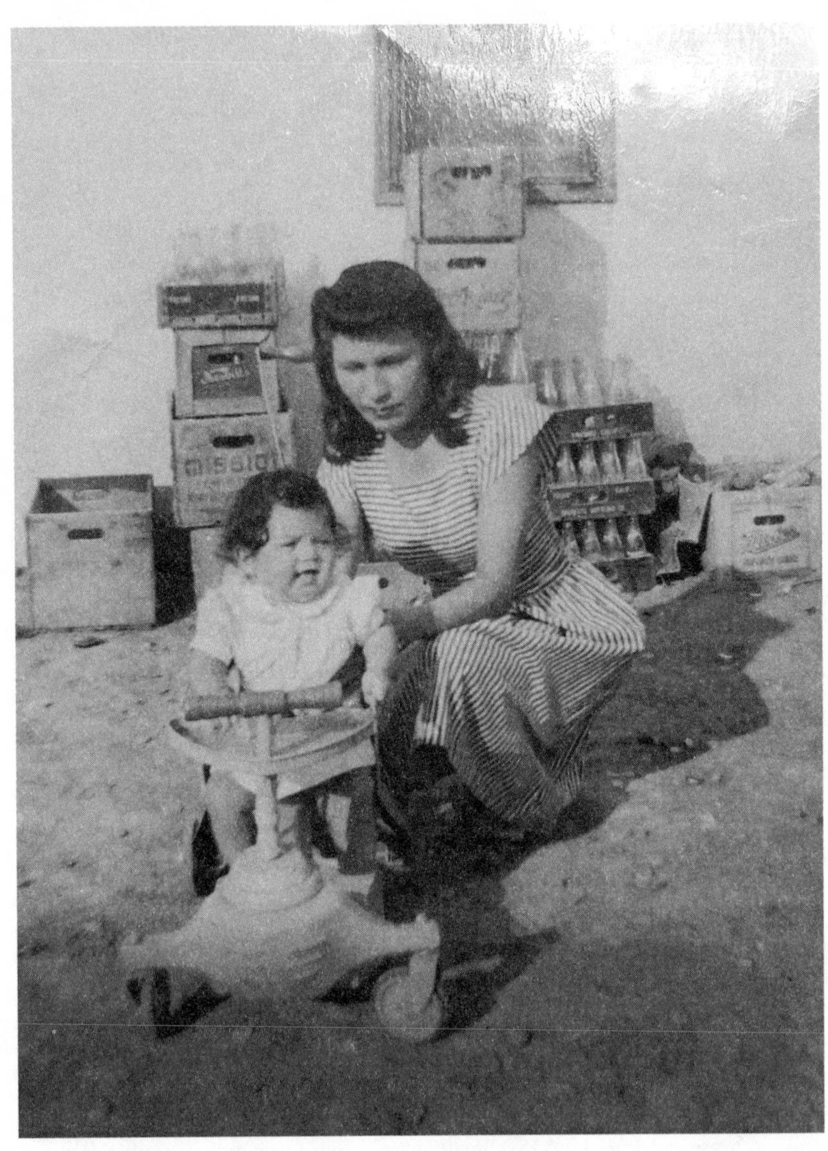

Bea with baby Alicia, Chowchilla, California, circa 1950.

III

DAMNATIO MEMORIAE

Death is the sanction of everything the storyteller can tell. He has borrowed his authority from death.

—WALTER BENJAMIN, *ILLUMINATIONS*

13

METHODOLOGY OF GHOSTS

2014

I'M HERE at UC Berkeley, at the Seminar for Latino and Borderland Studies. It's me and a roundtable of scholars: history, English, musicology, anthropology, and ethnic studies—a committee of mostly men. They've read the raw material that in a few years will become my book *All They Will Call You*. Papers shuffle, and they smile and nod. I take out the latest draft of my manuscript and set it down on the massive oak table. The smell of old books hangs in the air. It makes me nervous. I don't know if they'll get it. They stare at me through spectacles framed by graying heads. One coughs, drinks water. Silence. They begin. First, the accolades.

"This is fine work, Mr. Hernandez . . . may we call you Tim?"

"Of course," I say, taking a sip of water.

First, the historian. He brings up the media's omission of the Mexican passengers' names, and references "damnatio memoriae." Just like that, right out the gate. Everyone nods. Including me. I write the phrase down. Later I'll look it up. In ancient Rome there were many ways to condemn a criminal. "Damnatio ad bestias" was where they'd toss you to the lions and you'd be ripped apart before a crowd. The Romans were never short of creativity. But then there was the most dreaded of all condemnations, "damnatio memoriae," death of memory. After killing you they would chisel your name off all records, blotch your name off scrolls, and wipe away any sign that you ever existed. Erased eternally. Anyone who came looking for you a century later would be hard pressed to find anything more than a pale rumor. In effect, you were lost to history for good. "Everyone should be afforded the dignity of their name," the scholar comments. A phrase I've heard echoed since the beginning. I jot a few words down, things that seem important to remember:

Damnatio
Damnation
Damn Nation

It's the musicologist's turn. He's excited to speak, I can tell by the way he stares at me. The music buffs usually are. The music world has shepherded the story of the plane crash for more than fifty years. He says, "I've known of Woody Guthrie's song for a very long time and had always wondered about the Mexican passengers." Yes, yes, the others nod. "It's been a mystery decades in the making, and you've uncovered it." Yes, more nods. Soon they're all chiming in, and the conversation flows. They're curious about where I'm from. "What got you started on this forgotten piece of history?" They nod. "Yes, tell us . . . from the beginning."

And there it is again, "the beginning."

We talk about "beginnings" and spend the next hour going back and forth with questions they ask and answers I give. They offer suggestions, advice for directions I might take with this "raw material," or how they see the book taking shape. I welcome it all. I applied to the seminar looking to bounce these ideas off the very people who might later become my biggest critics. But instead of critics this committee turns out to be a supportive group.

My manuscript is scattered across the table now, and all the talk is spent, and it's just about over. But there's one more question. They're curious about my "methodology." The scholar asking this wants to know how much of my "methodology" I plan to let the reader in on.

"My methodology?" The word itself makes me cringe.

He explains, "The way in which you've gone about your research."

I know what he's asking. He wants to know how I've gone about locating these lost families. But the truth is I have no "methodology." Or if I do then it's rooted in two basic things I've followed since as far back as I can remember: curiosity and intuition.

But this is too abstract, too slippery. They want something concrete.

Okay then, here it is. Here's what I do: I write the names of all thirty-two passengers on scraps of paper, cut them into thin strips, and then scatter them across my kitchen table. Not unlike the way one uses a deck of tarot cards. I stand over the names, drink my coffee, or sometimes tequila, but lately mostly beer, and then I wait. That's pretty much it. It's just me and the names, without ceremony. I wait until one of them speaks to me. If nothing comes to me, I'll touch one of the names. Lift it to my face, press it against my chest, my forehead, the palms of my hands, my ear, hold it there for a few minutes. Sometimes I'll shuffle them around to see if a door will open. Maybe one will step across, demand to be picked up, or to have his or her name spoken into the air. So I speak their names, out loud, into the room. Kind of like one does in a séance, or when working with a medium. To invoke the names of the dead is serious business. There's a tradition in Latin America that when one calls out the names of the dead the community shouts back, "Presente!"—which is to say, "He or she is here with us now!" It is a powerful act when you experience it in the flesh. One hundred voices calling out "Presente!" in unison resonates deeply. This isn't merely a symbolic gesture. It's an actual invocation. So I invoke whenever necessary. Sometimes I get nothing from a name. There's a sense of vacancy, a void. But even a void has something to tell us. So I'll leave that name for another time. Perhaps another year, or another decade. But sometimes there's a strong pull. So I answer that pull. I lift the name up and begin asking it questions. Sometimes it replies. A word or phrase will appear in my head, and I'll type that into my search engine, and something will come up. Something always comes up.

Between 2010 and 2014, I became overwhelmed by how much information was coming at me; it was as if I had pried open a closet that belonged to thirty-two people and out spilled the mess of their entangled matters accumulated over seven decades. I was consistently up past midnight, obsessed with giving some organization to it all. Documents were funneling toward me from the four directions, phone calls and texts at all times of the day. It was clear the spirits weren't familiar with personal boundaries and had little, if any, consideration for my mental well-being. And if it wasn't the investigation, it was the media, especially in the weeks before and after we installed the memorial headstone. The Fresno diocese had issued a press release without my knowledge, and for months I was inundated with requests for interviews from outlets around the world. I quickly learned that not all attention was good. The first time I met the author Luis Alberto Urrea, he whispered to me, "Be careful, brother, the vampires are coming for you." I had no way of grasping the weight of his prediction at that time, but he couldn't have been more accurate. I began to wonder if the Aztec danzantes that performed a blessing at the headstone had jarred open a portal. I withdrew from sunlight and began numbing myself to it all. I began seeking escape routes, in discreet ways, drinking more and more, craving the anonymity that only a dive bar can offer, in whatever town or city I found myself in: Boulder, Albuquerque, Fresno, San Antonio, El Paso. The scars had already been accumulating long before this pressure found me. It was just the final spark that set things off. I was subconsciously sabotaging my relationships with people, especially those closest to me. My paranoia was festering, and I was constantly arguing with friends, and my circle was getting smaller by the day. I had a falling-out with my parents and excommunicated myself from their life for two years. It was convenient since I was now living in the seclusion of the Rocky Mountains, tucked away from the world.

It was in this dark period that, after a long, tumultuous relationship, my children's mother and I agreed it was time to go our separate ways. As I was trying to meticulously put together a fragmented piece of history, my personal life was falling apart. The two were linked without my knowing. At the start of this search my children were babies, and over the next thirteen years they'd somehow become old enough to tell when Dad was mentally not present. I was always physically present, and in fact prided myself on the kind of father I was becoming. But the truth is, in this particular slice of time, my headspace was wholly occupied by ghosts and memories, which haunt just the same. My mind toggled between two realms: drunken escapism and the constant reconciling of death. The theme of amputations, and the letting-go that follows, became my obsession du jour, a curse that infected every aspect of my life. I desperately wanted, needed clarity, but it was beyond my reach, so I went the other way. I was distrustful of everything and everyone, and booze was the only medicine strong enough.

This is where I was when Angela found me.

A practitioner of indigenous medicine, she invited me to her home in Berkeley, where she counseled me. "Have you been making offerings to the graveside and the crash site?" she asked.

"To be honest, I hadn't thought about that," I said.

In her own benevolent way, she glared at me as if I'd committed a major offense. She took a handful of tobacco from her pouch and motioned for me to take it. "You should always leave them an offering. Sprinkle a little tobacco or leave them a poem. Anything you like." I took the tobacco. She hesitated. "To be honest, you look really overwhelmed."

"You have no idea."

She stared at me through her thick-framed glasses and perfectly cut bangs, concerned.

"Ask them to get in line," she said.

I thought she was kidding. "You mean talk to them?"

She nodded. "They've been waiting a long time to tell their story, so they're crowding around you, like children. Just ask them to get in line. Let them know that you can hear them better if they come to you one by one."

She could sense my hesitation.

"They hear you, you know."

I hadn't told her about how they'd been visiting me. It was a relief to speak with someone about these things. It isn't the kind of subject you can just bring up at a dinner party, or to your therapist. Any time someone asked, "How's the search going?" I gave a ready-made reply: "It's going good, slow but good." And this lame response was usually enough to change the subject. But with Angela, this all just made perfect sense. Perhaps she was onto something. Perhaps this didn't have to be a one-sided conversation. I could speak with them. Why hadn't I thought of it before? I wasn't entirely at their mercy.

໑

But I am not there anymore, in the comfort of Angela's guidance. I am here now, at UC Berkeley, in the confines of academia, where reason and criticism are God. And the committee of scholars are staring at me, waiting for my response.

Methodology?

I gather the pages of my manuscript together. How to tell them that mine is in fact a "methodology of ghosts"?

14

THE UNEARTHING OF ██████████

I don't mind erasure if it is done by my own hand.
My choice. Write a word. Not the right word.
Turn the pencil upside down, erase.
—TERRY TEMPEST WILLIAMS, *WHEN WOMEN WERE BIRDS*

March 2014

I'M DELIVERING A KEYNOTE ADDRESS for the annual Cesar Chavez Fundraiser Breakfast in Stockton, California. It's held at the Mexican American Heritage Center, which is run by a woman named Gracie Madrid, who happens to be a cousin of my mom's. After hearing about my search, Gracie invited me to speak about the plane crash. Because Stockton was where the pilot run of the bracero program had occurred, I leapt at the opportunity. I brought a stack of paper slips listing the names of each of the victims and their hometowns in Mexico. At the bottom, I included my phone number and email. I carry these slips with me everywhere and place them in any open hand that accepts them. Since 2010, I've given away more than ten thousand of these slips. If you do the math it'll appear the odds are against me finding anyone this way. But intuitively it makes total sense. I'm convinced that this work won't be achieved by what's quantifiable, but instead by way of our "abuelita sensibility." The inexplicable logic of being in tune with our innate connection to the phenomenal world. What some refer to as "the law of attraction," our grandmothers have been manifesting since day zero.

Once everyone in the audience has a slip in their hand, I instruct them to read the names. And then I wait. Perhaps someone will recognize a name.

Perhaps they will be related. I wait and wait. But when everyone's faces stare blankly at me, I know nothing will come of it. Not this time.

After the event I sign books and thank Gracie for having me. Both of my parents are with me on this trip, and they are set to deliver me to the Sacramento airport tomorrow. The rest of this day is ours. But a storm is brewing and talk of rain is everywhere, so we take that into consideration. About an hour into our plan I receive a call. I don't recognize the number so I let it go to voicemail. I check the message:

"Mr. Hernandez, my name is ██████████, and I was at the breakfast fundraiser just now and I read the names you passed out . . . and I think a close friend of mine might be related to one of the passengers. Please call me."

Over the phone, ██████████ explains to me that her best friend, named ██████████, has both of the same last names as the passenger ██████████. And that she's from the same town in Jalisco. She says her friend ██████████ attends college in the Bay Area, but it so happens that she's visiting her mother in Stockton today. She arranges for me to visit ██████████'s house. At this point it's been four years since I began this search, and if she is right, then this will be the third family I've located so far. Thirty minutes later we pull up to the home that belongs to ██████████'s mother.

The rain has now rolled in, and a light sprinkle envelops us. I ask my mom to tag along, and together we scamper up the walkway and knock on the door. A young woman opens it. She looks to be in her mid-twenties, with light skin and blue eyes, and an air of innocence about her.

"Tim?"

"Are you ██████████?"

"Yes. My friend ██████████ called me."

"Thank you for agreeing to meet me on such short notice."

"Of course," she says, standing partially behind the door. I introduce my mom.

"Our apologies for coming unexpectedly," my mom says, shielding the rain with her hand.

"No, it's fine." She starts right in. "My friend called and told me something about a . . . plane crash?" She's hesitant. "To be honest, I'd never heard anything about it. So when she told me, I walked over to my grandma and said, Abuelita, do you know if we ever had a relative who died in a plane crash? His name was ████████ . . . and I didn't even finish saying his name when my grandma started crying, so I cried too, and that's when I knew we were related. My grandma said yes, ████████ was her uncle, and he did die in a plane crash a long, long time ago." She wiped tears from her face. "That's when I knew ████████ was right. But I'd never heard of it 'til just now." The rain begins to pelt us. "Oh, come inside, please come in." We step into her house and take our coats off. "My grandmother's actually visiting us from Mexico right now."

"Your grandma doesn't live here?"

"No, she just happens to be visiting. Crazy, right? Good timing."

████████ ushers us toward the living room. I begin to pull my audio recorder from my jacket, and when I look up, there, seated on the couch, is an elderly woman with the most luminous face, whitest hair, and bluest eyes. She takes one look at me and begins sobbing. I walk toward her, and she doesn't take her eyes off me. Her hands tremble. ████████ sits next to her grandmother and holds her. I sit next to my mom. We pay attention.

By the time I found Jaime and his brother Guillermo Ramírez, back in early 2013, their grief had, for the most part, been addressed. It had been two decades since they'd found the unmarked grave at Holy Cross Cemetery where the remains of their grandfather Ramón and their uncle Guadalupe were buried. A period during which, in their own words, they had "shared all the stories" of the men, with one another and with family. They believed, and still do, that had they not located the grave, they might've never felt okay enough to share the stories, which would eventually give them permission to let go and to heal. Which is to say, when I met the Ramírez brothers, I didn't have to face the consequences of my search.

It isn't until this very moment that I'm confronted with the very real and unresolved grief of a family who lost their loved one in "the worst plane crash in California's history." A wound that is still very much open. And now I've gone and stuck my finger in it. It doesn't sit well with me. I'm not equipped to navigate these emotions. I try to pay attention but my thoughts compound. What is my responsibility here? And what am I here for again? Author? Historian? Or am I just a man who knows something about loss in these parts of the world, seeking to mend my own past? If the former are true, then what is the trade-off? I am doubting myself again.

For the next hour, my mom and I listen to ████'s grandmother, who also happens to be named ████. She tells us the story of how her family had come to learn of her uncle ████'s death. It's an account that not even her granddaughter ████ has ever heard. Her cheeks drenched in tears, the elderly woman pushes through, giving us all her memory will allow. When she's done talking, she asks if I know where ████ is buried.

"Yes," I say, "he's buried just two and a half hours south of here, in Fresno." More tears slip from her eyes. I want to offer some light. I show her photos of the memorial service and the new headstone we installed, but all she does is nod and cry. She has no more words. What I've delivered to them isn't easy. Whatever they've had planned for their day, it's now tinted with this. My intuition tells me it's time to go and to give the family some privacy. I ask ████ if I can contact her in the coming days. She agrees.

"Let me walk you to the door," she says.

"Muchísimas gracias, Señora," I say to her grandmother. I look to ████. "I'm sorry for bringing your family this news."

"It's okay," she assures me. "Y que Dios te bendiga." She embraces my mom and me.

"We'll be talking with our family in Jalisco about this," she says. "I'll be in touch."

I mention a trip I have planned for Mexico. "It'll be in a few months," I say. "Please let your family in Jalisco know I'd love to visit them, if you think they'd be open to it. I mean, if you think that's something that can be arranged?"

"Yes, of course. I'll let them know."

15

THE PROMISE

January 2015

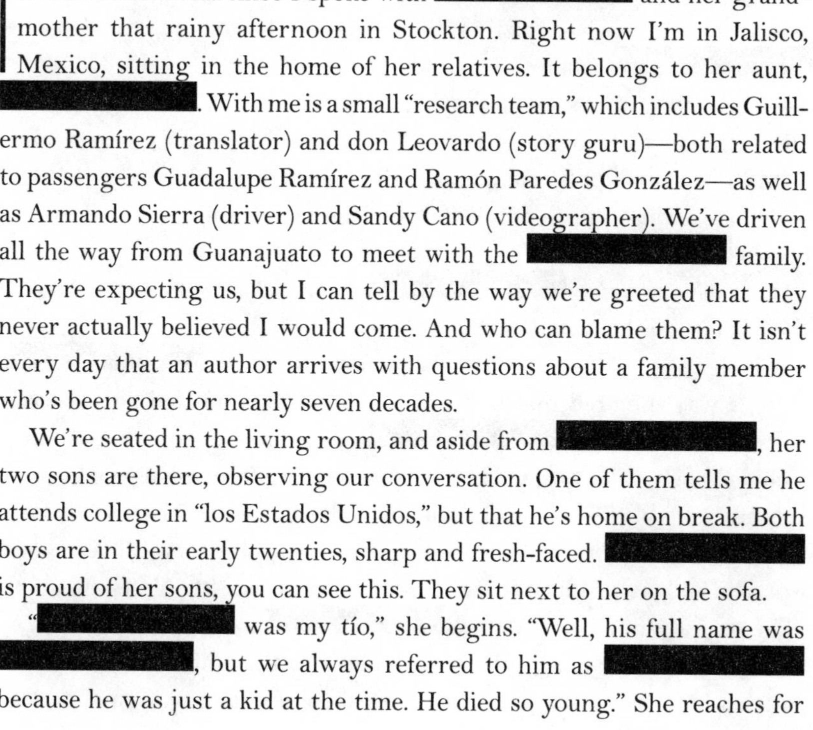

IT'S BEEN ALMOST A YEAR since I spoke with █████████ and her grandmother that rainy afternoon in Stockton. Right now I'm in Jalisco, Mexico, sitting in the home of her relatives. It belongs to her aunt, █████████. With me is a small "research team," which includes Guillermo Ramírez (translator) and don Leovardo (story guru)—both related to passengers Guadalupe Ramírez and Ramón Paredes González—as well as Armando Sierra (driver) and Sandy Cano (videographer). We've driven all the way from Guanajuato to meet with the █████████ family. They're expecting us, but I can tell by the way we're greeted that they never actually believed I would come. And who can blame them? It isn't every day that an author arrives with questions about a family member who's been gone for nearly seven decades.

We're seated in the living room, and aside from █████████, her two sons are there, observing our conversation. One of them tells me he attends college in "los Estados Unidos," but that he's home on break. Both boys are in their early twenties, sharp and fresh-faced. █████████ is proud of her sons, you can see this. They sit next to her on the sofa.

"█████████ was my tío," she begins. "Well, his full name was █████████, but we always referred to him as █████████ because he was just a kid at the time. He died so young." She reaches for a tissue and wads it in her hands. "I don't know very much about him, though. But I can tell you what little I do know."

"Whatever you remember is fine," I say. "It's an honor just to meet your family."

She says another relative who lives nearby might be better to speak with. He's older and has more memories of the time. She orders one of her sons to get him. A moment later they return, and now two more relatives have joined us. All admit they know little about ████████.

"What about ████████?" one of them suggests. "He might remember things."

The boy goes back out and returns with more family members. Within minutes the house is crowded with people, all wanting to see who has come asking questions about their long-lost relative, ████████, "el que murió en el accidente de avión," the one who died in the plane crash, they whisper.

But I didn't only come to excavate stories. I also came bearing information they didn't have. News about what happened to ████████. I hand them a folder with copies of the original newspaper reports, and a recent article depicting the memorial headstone, which bears ████████'s name.

"This is for you," I say. Guillermo hands the small box to ████████. "It's from Holy Cross Cemetery."

She opens it and lifts out a beautifully carved wooden crucifix.

"This is what the church would've given your family on the day they buried ████████."

Everyone is quiet. ████████ composes herself. The boys rest their hands on their mother.

Finally, she begins to tell us what she knows about ████████. How it was rumored that he was a wild and free-spirited kid who ran all over the streets of ████████, sometimes "getting himself into trouble," she recalls. She emphasizes that he came from good people: "Our families were well respected in this town. They still are." And while they grew up humble, they were never afraid to work. They were all very good workers, and law-abiding people, a point she stresses. She shifts direction. "This is the same house that ████████ was born in," she says, staring up at the ceiling. "We've just added to the house over the years, but that back part," she points over her shoulder, "is the original part of the house. Right here is where he was born." The family is proud. "Would you like to see it?"

She orders one of her sons to give us the tour. He takes us outside, and we walk around the perimeter to the back portion of the house. He points us to the adobe wall that still stands. "That's the original door," he says. I go to it and place my hands against it. "This is the door that ██████ would walk through each day," I say. He nods. We take a few photos.

Back inside the house most of the relatives have dispersed. It's now been two hours, and I can see that ██████ is anxious for us to leave. Sandy continues to capture our interview on video. She falls back, trying to be as unobtrusive as possible. ██████ eyes the camera.

I ask her if there's anything else she'd like to share. She's curious about the book I'm writing. I explain it's about the plane crash, and about the families that I can find. She wants to know if I'll be putting their story into my book. "I would like to," I say.

██████ turns to a relative and they quickly converse in a low whisper. There are things they'd rather we not hear.

Guillermo leans toward me. "I think she's afraid to talk with us." Don Leovardo senses this too. But he is in his eighties and has a seasoned understanding of people.

He clears his throat. "Two of my relatives were killed in the plane crash too," he says. Everyone quiets. "They were good men, well, not saints, but good men. And we have known Mr. Hernandez for a few years now, and he comes from good people too. I just want you to know this, so you feel comfortable."

██████ and her sons glance at one another. She looks at me. "Would you mind turning off the camera?"

"Of course not," I say.

Sandy turns off the camera and places it in its case.

"We understand the importance of your work, Mr. Hernandez." She pauses. "But the thing is, you see, we would prefer that you don't write about ██████ in your book."

The room is quiet. The research team looks at me. I nod, subtly. On the inside I'm trying to come up with a response that'll help put them at ease.

I know that whatever comes out of my mouth next is crucial to earning their trust.

"Of course, I respect your wishes," I say. "But may I ask why?"

"We just prefer that you don't." The look on her face is sincere, not at all stern.

Still, I have to try. "What happened to [redacted] was an injustice," I say, "and the way they handled his body after the accident even more so. Telling his story, with the input of you all, his family, is a way of correcting that."

She considers it. Her sons look to her. She glances at the few relatives who are still here, as if checking for their approval. They nod.

She's hesitant. "You see, when [redacted] was sent to the United States, our family felt it was a good thing, for his own protection. Because when he was here . . . well, he got into a fight and killed a man."

Don Leovardo removes his hat.

She continues. "He went to el Norte, just until things here calmed down."

Don Leovardo steps forward. "Señora," he says, "that's just how things were handled back in those days, there's nothing to worry about anymore. My tío Guadalupe also killed a man. And we're from a very small ranchito where everybody knows everybody. But those rivalries were so long ago, Señora, all those people are gone now. Times have changed."

The expression on [redacted]'s face dims. "I understand, but our family is well connected here. We are founders of this town."

Her son speaks up. "If you go into the municipio's office, in the lobby you'll see a mural of the founding fathers of [redacted], and our relatives' faces are painted on that mural."

There is dead silence now. What more can any of us say?

Before we leave, [redacted] makes me promise that I won't include any mention of [redacted] in my book. Nothing that will put the family back in the spotlight. It's a promise I intend to make good on. I remind myself that it's not about a book, it's about the people.

૭

As we drive away, I am left contemplating the promise. Was I too hasty to agree? Was there another way? Perhaps a greater writer would've never promised such a thing. What's a story without a name, or names, attached to it? What gets lost in the omission? What is gained? Until this moment, it never occurred to me that perhaps not all families want their stories told. It's possible that for some, the media's omission of their relative's name afforded them protection from their own circumstances, their own history. I am thinking of Bea Franco, and how she purposely omitted information about her third child. This complicates what I believed was my purpose. But the road is good for contemplation.

Armando drives in the direction of the sunset, a beeline toward our next stop, Guadalajara. And for the first time the research team is silent. The quiet is an invitation inward. I'm only now realizing how presumptuous it is of me to believe I'm somehow "giving voice to the voiceless." How altruistic. Christ. If I've been operating on this idea—and I have—it must stop now. Let's be real. This search isn't a selfless pursuit, or some unalloyed good, as many like to think that it is. I'm seeking something deeply personal here and attempting to find it in the families I meet. This search is in every way tainted by my own self-centered need to make sense of where this inherent pain I carry comes from. Perhaps there's solidarity in grief. In the way generations move on past the ruptures that perforate their story. In the way I hope to one day move on past my own. The projections are endless. Still, I'm wholly convinced that no one human can *give* voice to another. We are born with our voices intact. That is God-given. Not something bestowed upon us by another. We choose. We decide. And we tell our own stories when we are ready. When time has revealed its purpose to us and only us. When the conditions are right for us to do so. Not when an author comes knocking, or when a cause demands it. The [redacted] family has every right to protect themselves—books be damned! Their priority is in the here and now. Their story is a reminder that our loyalty is to the living, not the dead. I am learning.

16

THE HORSE STORY

It feels like a lot of things—like Judas, and horse, and love.

—NATALIE DIAZ, POET

꩜

IT WAS told to me during my first trek to Mexico in 2015 by don Miguel Pérez on the day before I was to leave Charco de Pantoja, Guanajuato. Guillermo had arranged for us to stay there, at his father-in-law's house, which acted as our home base during the time of our search. Most mornings, over a plate of eggs and beans that his daughter Dulce would prepare for us, I sat at the kitchen table, accompanied by don Miguel, who would seize the opportunity to feed me one story or another. The way he told stories reminded me of my grandpa, in that his anecdotes were either gravely serious or wildly mythical; there was no in-between. And they usually involved some lost memory, or article, or, in one case, the compensation still owed to him by the U.S. government for his work as a bracero. Days ago, he brandished a copy of his original bracero card, telling me that somewhere in Texas, someone was supposed to have been handling matters for the pension they were promised. He looked blankly at me, before shaking his head and stuffing his card back into his wallet.

On this, my last morning in Mexico, don Miguel shared with me one final story. It was a different kind of story. He chewed on his tortilla, then lifted his hat back on his head and swung his old eyes in my direction.

"Te han hablado del caballo?" he asked.

I shook my head.

He looked at Dulce, and she grinned at me.

"What horse?" I replied.

I couldn't tell if this was a setup for a joke or if he was being serious. He drank from his mug of coffee to clear his mouth. And then, in the slow and deliberate manner of an octogenarian, he began to tell me about this ancient "caballo raro" that was discovered in 1990, "right here in Charco de Pantoja, just a few blocks from here."

—On this particular morning, after days of torrential rains that had flooded el País de las Siete Luminarias, farmer Gabriel González Ledezma was tending to his field, to make sure it hadn't been washed away. As he began to walk home, down his usual path across the cobbled roads, he noticed a few stones had been dislodged, leaving immense holes. Out of consideration for his neighbors he began to put the rocks back. While doing this, he noticed something curious at the bottom of one of the holes. He pulled another stone back for a closer look, and realized it was the skull of a horse. The people of Charco prided themselves on their inherited knowledge of horses, and Gabriel particularly, which is why he also questioned if it was a horse at all. The thing looked slightly misshapen for a horse skull. He needed to find out. He pulled another stone out, and then another. And in a matter of minutes found himself staring down at a fully intact skeleton of a creature that appeared to be horselike but clearly was not a horse. The skull was slightly thicker than a normal horse skull, and the hind legs were longer than the front. It was a mystery.

By then a few other farmers had gathered around and were consulting one another as to what it might be. They disagreed, arguing about the possibilities. An hour later, still mystified, they scratched their heads, and Gabriel suggested the only logical move they had left: "Let's call La Maestra." The men unanimously agreed, and La Maestra was summoned.

Diana Garcidueñas was given the title of La Maestra by the people of Charco because she was among the few who had early on gone away and attended la Universidad de Guanajuato. But they also called her La Maestra because she was a schoolteacher and community educator who maintained her affiliations with la universidad. If anyone knew what to do with this mysterious horse skeleton, it would be her.

Minutes later La Maestra arrived to a large crowd gathered in the middle of the road. As she approached, a chorus of "Buenos días, Maestra" greeted her, and they parted and gave her room to work. She peered down into the hole for only a few seconds and speculated, nodding.

"Yes, this is a prehistoric fossil." When she came to her conclusion, chatter erupted. It was an exciting discovery. "I'll phone my colleagues at la universidad," she said. La Maestra left, and the people stood around in a large circle, proudly guarding the ancestral treasure.

No one can recall exactly how the conversation started, or who it came from, but someone suggested that this discovery was about to break open the long-standing myth that horses were brought here by Europeans, not at all native to this land. But the people of Charco know their history and know it well. They're aware that they dwell in the land of the Caxcanes, Otomís, Guachichiles and many other tribes, in the cradle of seven volcanoes, surrounded by pyramids and ceremonial relics that can be admired from practically any point in el Valle de Santiago. Not that they needed a fossil to prove what they themselves had already known, but for those who cared about such things as evidence and data, well, here it was. The skeleton of a prehistoric horse, preserved and intact, staring back at them. Whoever it was that La Maestra summoned from la universidad had better bring their best and brightest.

Within a few hours a vanload of paleontologists from la Universidad Nacional Autónoma de México arrived, salivating with excitement at the discovery. Anchoring the team was Dr. Óscar Carranza Castañeda, Mexico's leading expert on horse fossils.

> *Yes, I remember that day very well. I had first heard of the horse by way of my friend and colleague Juventino Martínez. I guess he got a call from someone in Charco de Pantoja, so he called me and asked if I'd like to go. It was me, Juve, Jesús, and I believe two Americans who went. We got there, and the people were very excited, I remember this. But I didn't speak with the community at all. Juve and Jesús spoke with the people, or rather, they had been speaking with them already, I don't know. But it seemed they knew one another, though I couldn't say. I never get involved in speaking with the community, I just don't. The reason for this is because . . . well, people have a way of creating fantasies, you*

> *understand? And I'm not there for any of that. My job is to be there for the bones, the fossils, so this is my focus when I go to a site. But I remember this specific horse. I remember all of my fossils. This one was a recent one, Equus cf. mexicanus, about 50,000 years old. It was from the Pleistocene Era. I remember it was almost fully intact, I believe it was just missing a front leg and some phalanges. From there we took the horse to UNAM, in Mexico City, where we cleaned it and assessed it. There aren't too many fully intact horses like that found around there, so it was pretty unique.*

It was quickly confirmed that what Gabriel González Ledezma had found that morning was in fact a prehistoric fossil. From the Pleistocene Era, aka the Ice Age. When volcanos were still active and woolly mammoths were king. The community cheered, and La Maestra thanked her colleagues who had driven an hour from Guanajuato city to make the identification. What happened next is where the mystery remains.

The paleontologists explained to the community that they needed to unearth the fossil so that they could further study it back at la universidad. Unearth the horse? The community was skeptical. The paleontologists shrugged. La Maestra was caught in the middle. The people of Charco were not having it. "Why not study it here?" they questioned. The paleontologists explained that they had special equipment in their labs, XYZ lasers and XYZ tools they needed to use under such and such conditions, and for this reason they needed to exhume the ancient horse. The people looked to La Maestra. She hesitated. In private, she conferred with the paleontologists. A deal was struck. The paleontologists agreed that once they had completed their studies of the fossil, they would return it to Charco de Pantoja. It was settled. There would even be a nice glass case in which they'd place it, with some signage, and it would forever be housed right here, in the heart of the community, among the people who felt, like all things that el País de las Siete Luminarias produced, that this ancient and sacred horse was their cultural and ancestral inheritance, their birthright. The people agreed.

In the October 1990 issue of *Earthwatch*, a magazine published by the esteemed Earth Corps, there is a photo of the unearthing. It is taken from a bird's-eye view, and it shows the community of Charco helping the paleontologists lift the horse out of its ancient bed and heave it into the van. In the photo we see families, men, women, and children, all gathered around, huddled close together, observing the spectacle. There appear to be nine men who are handling the fossil delicately. From this angle the fossil looks to be a couple feet off the ground, in the process of being lifted up, gently, carefully. Elderly women donning rebozos stand among the crowd, on their faces a gaze of concern. There is not a single smile among them, as they watch the almost unholy act of the horse's exhumation. Something doesn't feel right. This is especially clear on the face of a man who is wearing a white hat and white shirt, standing in the middle of the crowd with his hands crossed in front of him. Not even the children are smiling. A woman, with her arms folded, looks down defiantly at the situation. The energy in the air is still, as if everyone is holding their breath just seconds before one final heave, as the horse gets lifted into the van and carted away. After which, it will never be seen or heard from again—

Don Miguel is done telling me the Horse Story. He leaves it there a moment, hanging in the air for me to ponder. He wears the most serious expression. He turns to Dulce.

"Is your motorcycle working?" he asks. She nods. "Take Tim to see La Maestra."

"After breakfast," she replies. It's settled. Don Miguel has not taken his gaze off me.

"Maybe you can help us find the horse," he says. He takes a bite of his tortilla.

I'm caught off guard. "I wouldn't even know where to start," I reply.

"Well . . . you found us." He scoops a spoonful of beans into his mouth and continues eating.

The unearthing of "el caballo raro," Charco de Pantoja, Guanajuato, Mexico, 1990.

17

A BEGINNING

STAYING AT don Miguel's place, sharing meals and conversation, filled a void that had been left there by my grandfather Felix Sr.'s absence. In his final years, I would visit my grandpa in the town of Dinuba, my birthplace, and we'd sit outside, beneath his grapefruit tree, and talk. These informal "interviews" were my first foray into story gathering. However, my grandfather's experience was the flipside of don Miguel's.

My grandpa was never a bracero. Although he worked side by side with them, and considered many his close friends, in his own way he had disassociated himself from the workers who came from Mexico. It's possible it was born from his own resentment for his father, whom he hardly knew. José Encarnación Hernández, my great-grandfather, who was said to have been from Guanajuato, was never a presence in my grandfather's life. There is no memory of him. Which is to say that in the lore of our family, stories of José Encarnación do not exist. It is said that from the age of nine my grandpa hopped in the back of a truck with a bunch of campesinos and hit the road. The men, who were of no relation to young Felix, took care of him as one of their own. My grandpa was a lone wolf on an endless season. This at a time when the divide between two distant brothers—the Mexican bracero and the U.S.-born campesino—was the source of many misunderstandings.

By that time I was an adult with my own children, and because he was my last remaining grandparent, it felt imperative that I record my grandfather's testimony. During these "interviews" we talked about anything that crossed his mind. His upbringing. The family. And, of course, the subject that seemed to make him most uncomfortable—politics.

I once asked him for his opinion about the United Farm Workers movement, and specifically Cesar Chavez. He replied, "I was too busy working. While they were out protesting, I was trying to feed seven kids. Who was going to feed them? Pay my bills? Not Chavez. No, mijo." My grandfather prided himself on his ability to do the hard work that no one else wanted to do. It was this work ethic that moved him up in the ranks. He was trusted by many farmers on the circuit, from South Texas all the way up to northern Wyoming. Farmers knew who Felix Hernandez Sr. was, and they knew he did the work and didn't complain. For this reason, he was promoted to the rank of mayordomo, foreman, when he was still just a teenager. Later, he became the chief recruiter for farmers, hiring and firing men and transporting them to and from the fields. I have early memories of my grandfather walking up and down rows of grapes, showing pickers how to do it right, while shouting at others to get off their asses. This, long before the accident—

One normal afternoon, my grandfather is driving home after a long day in the fields. He's already dropped off most of the workers and is driving his sixteen-passenger van eastbound on the outskirts of Dinuba. There are just three more workers he still needs to drop off. As he approaches the intersection, he begins to slow to a stop, when a truck rams him from behind, forcing his van across the center divider and into oncoming traffic. To avoid smashing head-on into a vehicle he spins the steering wheel away from the road and launches his van into an irrigation ditch. The van hits nose first and my grandfather hears a loud pop that comes from his back. His van rolls over, end to end, tossing the other three passengers like sacks of potatoes. When it comes to a stop my grandfather calls out their names. Slowly each one answers. Two are trapped beneath seats, broken, and crying out in pain. Years later, when I ask him about it, my grandpa will tell me that he was just glad they were all alive. As for him, he'd broken three vertebrae in his back and was bedridden for weeks. And it's this accident that will mark the beginning of the end for my grandpa. Soon after, he isn't digesting food properly, so they harvest a piece of his stomach for testing. Resigned only to liquids, his dentures are removed. He eats less and begins to shrink. His diabetes worsens and his toe has to be amputated. Little by little I watch him disintegrate. Until finally, in the last year of his life, he's diagnosed with prostate cancer.

I went to visit him at the hospital in his final days. We spoke, and I recorded him with my small audio recorder. When he asked my aunt Hilda to get his turquoise watch from his pants, that's when I knew it would be the last time I saw him. He handed me the watch. "Here, mijo," he said, "it's your time." I was thirty-two years old. I took the watch from his trembling hand and put it on my wrist, where I've kept it ever since. Sitting there at his bedside, I recalled the countless accidents I'd seen firsthand all across the San Joaquin Valley. The backroads littered with roadside altars. I thought about the dusty crosses, and the small offerings left behind: balloons, plastic flowers, sometimes a photo, and often a name would be scrawled on the crossbar. So many names. I felt pulled by the mystery of each one. *Who are these friends all scattered like dry leaves?* What happens to their memory once the names fade? Perhaps it was the void left by the mystery of my uncle, baby Betito, and the fact that we could never find his grave. Each time we drove past these roadside altars my parents would cross themselves out of respect, a gesture I still practice to this day. In a matter of days my grandfather was gone. It was July of 2006. Four years before I would even hear about the plane crash at Los Gatos. But the concerns were now there, planted within me, germinating. Questions began forming. I returned to the writing. It was the only way for me to make sense of it. The night my grandpa died words came to me. I was hurting, and was angry, and I needed to interrogate, so I wrote a letter to the landscape. I sat down and furiously scribbled these questions into my journal:

San Joaquin Valley, why are your back roads stricken with altars,

and your plastic carnations entombed among deflated balloons?

What keeps the tattered photographs from disintegrating with the dew?

Who dies in the back of a narrow van, limbs splayed to the heavens?

Who survives? Who arrives first? Who will harvest the bodies?

Who will recall them in a dream?

How does one return the belongings?

When names fade, where do they go?

What Country will claim the purgatoried?

Who inherits the wreckage?

How deep is the ravine of a child's memory?

Are there two sides to the swallowtail's account?

How do we count the invisible?

Can angels scale border walls?

Who will open the gates for them?

Who denies them?

What manner of love is this?

18

VIRGIL

The task of unraveling my personal history, the flame that burns in the left side of my chest . . . an orphan is by nature a seeker of other selves, a night gazer with fire in the blood.

—JUAN FELIPE HERRERA, *MAYAN DRIFTER*

ଡ

BY THE time I was eighteen he had become my mentor by default, advising me through all the bullshit that came with young adulthood. Always there with good and bad advice, or a crass joke that made everything seem lighter. He knew how to put things into perspective for me.

Virgil had been living with us off and on over the years, dealing with his own ghosts and trying to get his life in order. He had a wife now, and a newborn son, and they rented a place a few miles from our house. Still, when things turned chaotic, as they often did, he retreated to the home of "the only mother he ever knew," Chita. During the longer stretches, while occupying the room across the hall from mine, he evolved into more of an older brother to me than an uncle. We hung out often, watched sitcoms on television, did yard work, and clowned around a lot, in mostly adolescent ways. There's a photo of us, taken on the day of my high-school graduation, and he has his arm around me, like a proud uncle, both my parents at our sides. It would be another year before I would consider the possibility that I was also filling a void in Virgil's life. Without realizing it, I had become something of a surrogate for the firstborn son he once lost, years before. Of course, at the time the photo was taken, I knew very little about his life in New Mexico. It never occurred to me to ask. Had I asked I might've learned that Virgil too had once gone on his own search—

꩜

The story goes that Virgil cheated on his first wife, so she took little Virgil Jr. and left him. No one has ever actually told me that this is what happened, but somehow it's the story that sits on the shelf of my memory. It could be that I overheard it while eavesdropping on my mom's conversations, perhaps one of the many between her and her baby brother. They were always talking in the kitchen, Mom cooking something, Virgil at the table, like a grown son. I can see him seated there, white tank top, chin tilted up, bravado on full display, voice booming, arms waving in the air. Every time he spoke it was like he was conducting an orchestra.

Long before his California years, he was a young father, barely eighteen, and had a beautiful wife named Irma—a Mexicana from Palomas, Chihuahua, just on the other side of the border from Columbus, New Mexico. Together the young couple had a baby boy, whom they named Virgil Jr. One morning Virgil leaves for work, and when he returns home there's a note on the kitchen table waiting for him: *Cabrón, I know you've been seeing another woman. Desgraciado! You don't deserve us!* Who actually knows what the note said, but it's easy to imagine. Regardless of the message, Irma and Virgil Jr. are nowhere to be found. Virgil knows he's done wrong, there's no justifying it. He knows that Irma is a good woman. I overhear him say this to my mom once or twice. He admits she deserved better. But to take his only son away? This is the singular act that drives Virgil mad. She's aware of his past, the resentment he holds for having been orphaned at such a young age due to the untimely death of his mom. She knows he has every desire to be a father, maybe not a great one, but at least one who's present, the kind he himself never had. The thought of Virgil Jr. growing up without him stokes a desperate fire in his chest, the anger constantly churning beneath the surface. The ghost of his father, Alejandro, looms.

꩜

Recently, while at a family barbecue in El Paso, I witness our relatives debating where exactly Virgil searched for his son, Virgil Jr., during those years—

"He went into Mexico, deep in there, to try and find his little boy."

"No, no, it was just to Palomas, because that's where little Virgil's mom was from."

"I wouldn't doubt it, Virgilio was street smart, cabrón para buscar lo que necesitaba. He could find anything and anyone."

"He also went to Albuquerque, and then to Colorado too, I remember that because he came to ask me for advice."

"That's true, because I went with him on one of those trips . . . to Colorado."

"What's in Colorado?"

"I guess she had family there or something."

"He looked for them for years, at least three or four."

"Pobre Virgilio, I swear he went everywhere searching for his little boy."

꩜

Sometimes, usually at the tail end of a family barbecue, once everybody had left and he had several beers in him, Virgil would open up a little and tell me about his son. What he remembered of him, anyway. Little by little it would leak out.

"My boy was smart, mijo—" he'd say, throwing back a swig.

"He was riding a bike before he could walk—"

"He would be about your age now—"

"He had my hair and good looks—"

"I bet you'd get along good with him—"

And then he'd sit quiet for a moment. Sip his beer.

It was clear that Virgil had stopped giving himself permission to hope long ago. He'd come to terms with the loss. Witnessing his desperation was working on me without my knowing it. By the time of my high-school graduation it had been more than ten years since he'd last seen Virgil Jr.

꩜

I have amassed an archive of memories of my uncle, all of them occurring before the time I turned twenty-one. The memories and snapshots in my head are all jumbled, but there are two that I have no problem distinguishing from the rest.

My favorite happened in 1994—

He's fresh out of the shower, combing his hair. His energy is light, like I've never seen him before. On his bed is a duffel bag, packed for a trip. I ask him where he's going. He says, "To see my boy." He says it as if he himself can't believe he just said it. He's found Virgil Jr. In this moment I don't think to ask how. I'm unable to fully grasp the weight of what this means for him. Not now, anyway. I won't know the love a father has for his child until my own come into this world. But right now I'm still eighteen.

"I'm going to his high-school graduation," he tells me, his eyes radiant.

"Where?"

"He lives in Blythe."

"In the desert?"

"Can you believe that? I've passed Blythe more times than I can count. Sometimes the shit we look for is right under our noses."

"I'm happy for you, tío."

"We're supposed to have breakfast the next day."

"That's awesome," I reply, a hint of animosity in my voice.

He asks my mom what he should wear for the graduation. She loans him one of my dad's blazers. It's slightly big on him but it'll work. He's nervous, excited. He asks my mom for advice about what he should say and do, how to act.

She tells him, "Just be yourself."

"That's terrible advice," he says, jokingly. I agree. He takes a jab at me.

That night he loads his pickup truck and I watch him drive away, his taillights fading into the dark. But this is not my favorite part of the memory—

This is:

Days later, Virgil returns home from visiting his son in Blythe. He looks melancholy and slightly defeated. He tosses his duffel bag onto his bed. He's quiet. And then—

"My boy's a goddamn genius," he says, his eyes searching for words. "That kid knows all about basketball and sports, and music too . . . you can ask him anything and he knows about it. And he reads books, goddamn! And he's handsome, just like his dad—" He laughs, and goes on and on, in a stream of consciousness, dumping every thought that has accumulated during the last several hours while driving home, his expression childlike. In all the years I've known my uncle, I've never before seen this look on him.

"How was breakfast?" I ask.

"He couldn't make it after all." He hesitates. "It's okay, though, he's busy, he's a young man now, I know how it goes."

"Sorry, tío," I say.

It doesn't seem to bother him. Or not that he lets on. After ten years of searching, he's found his boy, and nothing can come between them now. His firstborn son and his newborn son are both in his life. As a father he feels whole again. A redeemed man. Over the next few weeks my uncle is joyful, bouncy even. Where once there was a general defeat about him, there's now a glint of pride and optimism in his eyes. It's a noticeable difference. We all see it. But no one wants to call attention to it. Because it's fragile, delicate, butterfly-like. So we hold our breath, tiptoe around it, fearing that one slight move, one misstep, might scare it away.

19

DRINKING WITH GHOSTS

I **WAKE UP NAKED**, hungover, hot. It's become routine. Especially in the year following the separation with my children's mother. The cadaver of unfulfilled dreams haunts me. I yearn to reach back and resuscitate, live there again. I yearn to lunge forward and forget where I've been. I yearn to be touched. A phantom limb will itch. I scratch it with booze. A flood of memories and fragments. They shadow me. I imagine it as akin to what the poet William Butler Yeats called "the gyres." A historical vortex consumes me. Things are coming undone. My mind is on loop. A replay of our worst years. And then our best ones. We laugh hard and cry harder. We argue, shout, and agree that we've had enough. She moves to California. I stay in Texas—with the kids.

I am thrown into the frightening realization of what my grandfather Alejandro was up against when my grandmother died. The task of raising children alone in the desert will tease out your greatest self-doubt. The fear is crippling. Some days it wins. Some days it doesn't. I'm only raising two. My grandfather was left with six. His became a world without gravity. I keep his story close to anchor me. A talisman. I won't let this desert beat me. I commit to drinking more water, meditating longer, and doing one hundred push-ups a day. But not today. Today I am in California, conducting research, while staying at a friend's house.

Today I will turn my face away from the sunlight. A thin layer of sweat gathers on my upper lip, and I can smell the alcohol emanating from my body. My eyeballs are on fire and my brain is pounding. My stomach churns between nausea and loneliness. These are days best spent between the pages of books—my loyal friends.

No matter how much I drink, it never leaves. There aren't enough ghosts to distract me.

I write these words down in my journal. Speak them out loud to myself. Proceed with caution.

I'm doing it again, counting the years I've stayed numb. Since I was eighteen. The majority of my life. Weekend after weekend. I've become strategic at knowing when and where to do it. It's in the gaps. And it requires calculation. Timing. Because I am, after all, a responsible man. I tend to my babies and my job. But then there are the gaps. In that order. The problem is that it's only within the gaps that I have time to conduct my search for the passengers of the plane crash. So sometimes both must happen simultaneously, drinking and searching. At times I wonder if the two are linked. Like archenemies, each reliant upon the other for its own existence. Perhaps when I find what I'm searching for I won't need to drink anymore.

Last night I was at my best friend David's house, in Visalia, fifty miles from where I'm staying. A storm rolled in. I pounded beer and guzzled whiskey until I blacked out. Without saying a word to anyone I left the party. Ghosted. It's the only way I ever leave anywhere these days. I drove off in the rain on "the most dangerous stretch of highway" in the United States—Highway 99. I remember it was pouring, and then a diesel blaring its horn. Bullets of rain bashed my windshield. I remember looking out of one eye. And then I drifted off to sleep. That's how it happens, doesn't it? That's when it happened. I slammed open my eyes and lunged for the steering wheel. I stomped my foot down on the brakes, but it was beyond my control now.

I expected to feel my truck skid across the highway, or see the diesel's headlights, but when that didn't happen, I sat upright and took inventory of my body. My truck was somehow, inexplicably, parked at a rest stop. And there was no rain. The only evidence was a few droplets on the windshield. My truck was turned off, and the keys had been placed neatly atop the dashboard. I had blacked out. I don't know for how long. It's surreal how during a blackout the body can still function with your phantom at the wheel. Is it crazy to believe that this was an intervention of the angelic? Maybe. There are other explanations, sure. But none feels truer. I know the state I was in. I heard a diesel horn blare at me. I woke to the sun peeking over the Sierra Nevadas. I stuck the keys into the ignition. My hand was trembling. I put the truck into drive and started off. I stayed in the slow lane and dragged quietly up the highway, acutely aware that I was now moving inside the eggshell of a miracle.

Lying in bed, I recall what Angela told me about making offerings to the spirits of the passengers. And since then, that's what I've done. I've made offerings at the crash site in Los Gatos Creek. I've made offerings at their gravesite, even offerings at the cemeteries in their hometowns in Mexico—in el panteón de Charco de Pantoja, Guanajuato, in el panteón de La Estancia, Zacatecas, and in el Rincón de Parangueo. I've even made offerings at Martin Hoffman's grave at the Navajo burial grounds in Rough Rock, Arizona, where I was warned against going because of *chindi*, the dark spirits. But I wanted to make sure I covered all my bases. The offerings consisted of sage, tobacco, and poem-prayers. At each offering I made a point of asking for their permission. Permission to enter their past. Permission to enter their families' lives and excavate the stories. It feels like the right thing to do.

"You have to keep yourself protected," Angela advised. She used the analogy of a caracol, the snail's spiral shell, as a way of explaining it to me.

"You see, it always circles back, getting tighter and smaller with each passing," she said. "And this spiral is made up only of people you trust, and important spaces or stories you return to again and again over time, and it protects as it surrounds you, but it's never closed off. That's the key. The caracol stays open-ended because it's an invitation." This idea felt right to me. I wondered how much all the drinking had closed me off without my knowing. How much I'd compromised. Like with all modes of communication, a clear channel means better reception. But a compromised network is a playground for hackers. And there are spirit-hackers. See: *mal de ojo*, or Italian *malocchio*, or the Greek *mati*, or the Turkish *nazar*, or the Egyptian Eye of Horus. In all cultures, dangerous entities loom. I convinced myself. I needed to bring as much clarity as possible. I needed to stop drinking.

Driving toward Fresno, I thought about the idea of circling back toward some beginning, a new beginning, or perhaps just another beginning. I had to return to the source. I headed straight to Holy Cross Cemetery, back to the headstone. It was early and the cemetery was still closed. I jumped the fence and walked over to the headstone. I sat down in the wet grass and searched for words. A small crop duster flew directly overhead, on its way to a field. The morning traffic was fading in. My eyes were heavy; I was still drunk. I had four hours before I was to go speak with the Ramírez family, but I was in no condition for it. I even tried forcing myself to vomit, to get it out of my system, but nothing helped. I placed my cheek on the headstone's cool granite. I could feel myself drifting off to sleep. I forced myself to sit back up. I sat still, alone with my thoughts. I was desperate to understand how and why my life had become such a wreck. And even more desperate to understand how it might all be tied to this search. Over the last several years I had gotten good at investigating others. Perhaps it was time I turned the investigation inward. Words came to me. I spoke them out loud. To the names etched on the headstone. To the sky. To the silent grass. And to the ones I believed carried me to safety last night—

I don't understand my purpose in all this . . .
what's the point? I know . . . there's a pain
inside of me, old wounds I haven't healed . . .
is this what this is all about? I'm lost. I feel lost.
Help me, Grandma, help me, Grandpa. Help me see.

20

INHERITANCES

1993

I CAN'T EVEN OPEN MY EYES because I'm that stoned. Jesse and I leave the party. I'm nineteen, and behind the wheel now, and we're passing a fifth of vodka between us. I exit Highway 198 and bounce over an island divider on Lover's Lane. A Visalia Police Department cruiser spots me and pulls me over. The officer approaches my car, hand on his gun. By now I've had two incidents where police have pointed guns at me and I'm scared as shit. He's at my window. I roll it down. He asks if I've been drinking. I mumble something, then attempt to pull my driver's license out, but I'm fumbling. I hand him what I think is my license, but it's a photo of my girlfriend Alejandra.

"Step out of the vehicle," he says. I can't find the handle. He opens the door and I spill out onto the pavement. He scrapes me off the ground and props me against the car. He tells Jesse to get out. Jesse does as ordered. We've both been here before, we know how to act, what to say, what not to say. The officer gives me a sobriety test, and I fail. I can't even stand up. He tells Jesse to take a walk, and Jesse does. I'm now cuffed and in the back seat of the cruiser. I'm now inside the processing room of the Tulare County Jail. My body is scrutinized for scars and tattoos. A needle stabs my left arm. A mug shot is taken. A metal door slams. I black out. "Hernandez," a voice shouts. I'm up again. The metal door slams. I make a phone call. And then I'm released into the shock of morning light. I begin walking home.

When I arrive, Virgil is washing his pickup truck in our driveway. He takes one look at me and he knows. "Where's your car?" he asks. I shrug. He shakes his head.

"Is my mom pissed off?"

"I reckon you go inside and find out yourself."

Virgil always uses the word "reckon." The only brown man I've ever heard use it. I wonder where he picked it up from. His presence calms me a little.

I go inside and lie in my bed, pass out. I hear my mom enter the house. She shouts my name. I sit up and she slams open the door to my room.

"Where's your car?"

"It's impounded," I say.

She's furious. She goes to find my dad. He comes in and asks me the same question.

"Impounded," I repeat.

"Were you drinking?"

I say nothing. They stare at one another.

I'm nauseous. I bolt to the bathroom and vomit into the toilet.

෧

It's the afternoon of my sixteenth birthday. I'm skateboarding with friends during lunch break, just a few blocks from Redwood High School. The bell rings and my friends stay behind, but I hurry back. I decide a shortcut through the alley is quickest. I'm skating fast to avoid being late. As I emerge from the alley a green sedan skids to a stop in front of me. I jump off my board before it hits me. Two men leap out, guns drawn. They want to see my hands. They're dressed in plain clothes, and no badges are flashed. I begin to tremble. They jam me into the back seat of their car. I'm confused. A shotgun is mounted between their seats. It doesn't yet occur to me that they might be cops. Not until one of them gets on the CB and staticky words are spoken. It sounds urgent. The tires squeal and the car speeds onward. "What did I do?" I ask, my voice quivering. They ignore me. We screech to a stop and both men jump out of the car and run to help a gang of uniformed officers brawling with two guys. In a matter of seconds, the guys are cuffed and lifted onto their feet. Two older white men with bloodied faces. I watch it all from the back seat. When the commotion is over, one of the officers points at me, and another, his superior, shakes his head. How a lone brown boy can be mistaken for two old white men is beyond me. But this is Visalia.

Its reputation persists. The officer opens the door to let me out. "Go back to school," he says. And that's it. No explanation, no apology. My legs are still trembling. I can't skate. So I walk. The entire way back to school I feel a swell of adrenaline coursing through my veins, from my wobbly knees to my fingertips. I feel it in my chest and fluttering in my stomach. I can't calm myself. It's a sensation I'm not familiar with, and it feels like something has broken inside of me. A glitch in the nervous system. As I approach campus, I don't want anyone to know I've been crying, so I hide behind a tree to try and compose myself before I walk into the office. With each step I'm now aware that I'm forcing these tremors deep down inside my body until they disappear. But they never will.

Because that same year it happens again. Me and my friends leave a party after getting into an argument with some college guys. Someone calls the Visalia Police Department and gives them a description of my car, saying we "flashed a gun." On Visalia's main drag we're pulled over, and within seconds a phalanx of cops has us surrounded. Six or seven guns pointed directly at us. They speak through a bullhorn. Traffic stops to watch. People emerge from their houses. I'm behind the wheel so they deal with me first. I'm made to get out slowly, place my hands on my head, and walk backward toward them. An officer slams me down onto the pavement and cuffs me. I beg them to put their guns down. They won't listen. "Where's the fucking gun?" he shouts at me. "We don't have a gun!" I shout back. He pulls me up by my arms and tosses me into the back seat of a cruiser. I watch as they do the same to my friends. One of them, the last one, is stuck in his seatbelt and can't get out. The cops begin shouting at him. People are staring. I feel lightheaded. From the back seat I yell, "Don't shoot anybody! We don't have a gun!" That night no one gets shot. They take us to the station and release us to our parents. No gun was ever found. I was sixteen. And now the tremors remain with me indefinitely.

૭

I'm glad you pulled me over or I could've killed somebody.

This is what the report claims I told the officer. I don't remember saying this. But I don't remember not saying this. I would've said anything to keep in the good graces of the Visalia PD. When he cuffed me I'm sure I said, "Thank you." The report says blood was extracted. My blood alcohol content was 0.210. Technically alcohol poisoning.

The judge looks at my BAC and repeats the number out loud, in the courtroom, for all to hear. A man dressed in orange and wearing handcuffs chuckles. The judge peers at me from behind his bifocals and doesn't blink when he says, "Two hundred hours of community service." I think I'm off the hook. But then he says, "And you can either pay two thousand dollars or serve thirty days at Bob Wiley Detention Facility."

The tremors rise up in me.

"Thirty days?" I repeat. The courtroom is silent. The judge is emotionless.

It's at this moment that I remember my dad is the new manager of a finance company and now makes decent money. It's been years since he was a farmworker. I've never been more grateful for my father's ambition than in this moment. I look to him.

"Do we have two thousand dollars?"

He side-eyes me, and I can't tell if he's sympathetic or upset. He shakes his head. "I do," he says. "Do you?"

I hope he's kidding. But he's not. I turn my eyes back toward the judge. "I'll serve the time, your honor."

I'm given fourteen days to turn myself in.

൭

The morning I arrive at Bob Wiley Detention Facility, there's a line of guys ahead of me. We're each given brown-bag lunches, then released into the yard. Officers eyeball us, but mostly everyone ignores us. I remind myself it's minimum security, nothing like the movies. Still, I sit on a bench and try my best to not look like a target. I puff my chest out and put a scowl on my face. It's pathetic. I'm sure I'm not fooling anyone. The sun is bearing down on us. I sit and do nothing. Stare at the ground. I look at my watch and see it's only been five minutes. I'm ready to go home. I've learned my lesson, I swear. But the look on everyone's faces assures me no one cares. The gopher holes here are ridiculously large. Too bad they're not large enough for me to escape through. I'm thinking about how to make myself invisible when a voice calls out, "Hernandez?" I look over my shoulder. It's Cody, a guy I went to continuation school with. He's a slacker who comes from money. A real asshole. I've always disliked him. But right now I'm glad to see him.

"What the fuck are you doing here?" he asks.

"DUI."

"Goddamn."

TULARE COUNTY
SHERIFF
RECORDS DIVISION
BOOKING PHOTO

ID#: **210843**

NAME: **HERNANDEZ, TIMOTHY NMN**

DOB: **02-16-1974**

RACE: **HISPANIC** SEX: **MALE**

HEIGHT: **510** WEIGHT: **170**

BUILD: **SLENDER** DOA: **09-30-1993**

HAIR COLOR: **BROWN** LENGTH: **SHORT**

EYE COLOR: **BROWN** GLASSES: **No**

FACIAL HAIR: **NONE** SKIN TONE: **MEDIUM**

S/M/T LOCATIONS: **HEAD**

S/M/T DESCRIPTIONS: **NONE**

CASE#:

CHARGES: **23152BCVC**

The mug shot I don't remember taking, Tulare County Sheriff's Department, 1993.

"You?"

"Stole some shit. Expensive shit." He laughs. "Cannot fucking believe you're in here, man."

"I can believe you're here," I say, attempting to joke.

"Fuck you."

In this moment I want to believe that everything's going to be okay. Cody is here. And somehow he's managed to survive. It can't be that bad. I look at my watch. Only twenty minutes have passed. I still have the rest of this day, and twenty-nine more to go.

I'm what they call a "weekender." My time falls under the "cakewalk" category. Still, I'm given jobs to do during the day. And when evenings come we all stand at the gate and listen to the officers read numbers from a list. If your number is called you go home early. The guys call it a "fourteen-day kick." Time off for good behavior, that type of thing. By the end of this first day I'm already standing at the gates praying to hear my number.

࿊

While everyone passes time doling out one hustle or another, I sense there's a layer of psychology working underneath us all. Even at this age I already recognize a dehumanization process unfolding. Of course, I won't learn these words until much later. I only know that it feels vaguely similar to the run-ins I've had with the Visalia PD. Standing at the zero end of a loaded Glock while a man with a badge shouts false accusations at you is a feeling you don't easily forget. You become keenly aware of how fragile your life is, momentarily. Your perception of Self instantly changes, causing a permanent shift in your DNA. From here on out, any time a gun is flashed the tremors return.

By the fifteenth day my number is called and I'm out. But it's enough time to leave the imprint that every boy of color comes to learn eventually—your body isn't as much yours as you once believed it to be. Being referred to by a number was just the start of it. I won't soon forget the expressions on the officers' faces, and how they spoke down to us. Even light banter had teeth. The foods we ate were served the way they were in elementary-school cafeterias, in brown bags, mystery meat, kid-size milk boxes. I would later learn the word for it, "infantilized." Denied our maturity, which is to say our experience. All of it designed to make you aware that you no longer belonged to you. The "you" you once thought so highly of, thought was so important, gone. Disembodied. Without heart or flesh or family or history—except that which they choose to remember you by. It's here where I first grasp that to be nameless is to be storyless. And to be storyless is to be disposable.

This too was some kind of a beginning.

IV

IN CONSIDERATION OF THE CARACOL

They sent sign after sign. Sometimes if I stopped writing and drew one hand over another my hands smelt of violets or roses, sometimes the truth I sought would come to me in a dream.

—WILLIAM BUTLER YEATS, *A VISION*

21

METHODOLOGY OF GHOSTS

WILLIAM BUTLER YEATS held séances in his house. He wasn't alone. He recruited the help of his wife Georgie. Yeats believed that when it came to writing, nothing was off-limits. But his approach was unique. Rather than writing *about* dead people, why not just interview them directly? Why not invite the dead to speak for themselves? But there needed to be a channel, a medium. Because a woman's cycle is aligned with the moon and other celestial bodies, at the time (and still) it was widely believed that women had access to the astral plane that just wasn't naturally available to men. And so it goes. Yeats convinced Georgie to be his personal medium. The arrangement was that Georgie, with pen and pad before her, would perform a ritual to summon the spirit of the dead, and when a connection was made and the dead began to speak, she would transcribe the message verbatim. Material that Yeats would then go on to publish under his name and only his name. Eventually he would come to call this process "automatic writing." It would gain popularity, but not without scrutiny. The arrangement raised an ethical question that persists to this day: If the whole thing was Yeats's idea, but his wife Georgie was the medium, and therefore the writer, and the words of the writing itself came directly from a ghost or a spirit, then who was the true author of the writing? Which is to say, who holds the copyright?

A medium named Geraldine Cummins, whom Yeats consulted with at times, would eventually settle this argument once and for all. She too had been hired—in her case by a man named Frederick Bond—to generate some "automatic writing" in correspondence with a spirit named Cleophas. In each session, Cleophas's messages were consistently addressed to Frederick. And because he was the one who hired Cummins, he argued that the writing she generated belonged to him. But Cummins wasn't having it. Not after she'd seen the way Yeats omitted Georgie's name from the cover of his book *A Vision*, which was largely sourced from Georgie's personal contact with the spirit world.

In the court case *Cummins v. Bond*, it was determined that the author is the one who converts the message of the supernatural into readable language. Therefore, the courts ruled, the person wielding the pen is the author and holder of the copyright. But the outcome of this copyright law didn't stop arrangements between authors and mediums from taking place. In fact, it only popularized them. More female mediums began generating writing for the male authors who hired them, with the agreement that the male author would publish the work under his name only. The only difference was that now it had to be consensually agreed upon and formalized with a contract signed by both parties. This practice continues to this day and is far more accepted than ever before. But now we call this arrangement "ghostwriting," since it was originally based on correspondence with ghosts.

But that's not the part that gets me.

What gets me is that during the court proceedings the one inarguable fact was that this precedent was based on people—writers in this case—communicating with ghosts. As if it was common knowledge among everyone involved, including the courts, that the dead do in fact speak.

I carry this story in my pocket like an amulet, to remind me that the history is there. Writing has always been a portal for the dead. I am not alone in this. A century ago, the Spanish poet Federico García Lorca introduced us to the name for when the angel and the muse speak through us in a surge of inspiration—duende! *Through the empty archway a wind of the spirit enters,* he wrote. In this way, if we are attuned to it, the writing becomes something more than just words on paper; it acts like a seismograph registering what lies beneath. The truth is, I don't know if these things apply to my search, but I don't know that they don't. I have to stay open to all of it. I'm trying to make sense of how to put these things together. I am turning to the history, digging up the stories. I am leaning into language. I am learning.

22

VIRGIL

I'M IN my bedroom, lying on the floor, painting. This is all I do at nineteen. More than a place to sleep, it's my studio. Everything is colored and scribbled on—my walls, ceiling, mirrors, the carpet. It's my sanctuary. I find solace in the aloneness. I always have. But it's a double-edged machete. I crave solitude. But also, I am lonely. At this time, painting is the only thing that makes sense to me. Writing is nowhere on the horizon. But in this particular memory, I'm brooding over a job offer that I desperately want to accept but can't. Because I can't get over the fear. I'm in this pathetic state when Virgil opens my door and peeks his head in. He's carrying his baby son, Eric, in his arms. He stares at all the paintings scattered across the room.

"Your mom told me the prison wants to hire you to teach art to inmates?"

I mumble something.

"How much are they gonna pay you?"

"Nineteen an hour," I groan.

"Fuck, you better take it."

"I can't go back into those kinds of places."

He laughs. "You gotta do it. That's too much money to say no to."

I don't respond, wishing he'd just drop it.

"You can't be scared when a door like that opens, mijo. You got talent, boy. You better do it."

Baby Eric grows fussy, and Virgil tends to him. They leave my room.

A year later, we're cruising past the Visalia Mall; Alejandra's behind the wheel. The mall is undergoing an expansion and it's under construction. I see his white work truck parked in the middle of it. I recognize his toolbox in the bed of the truck. Virgil is standing a few feet away. I ask Alejandra to drive closer. I can see Virgil is eating his lunch. And by the way he's holding it in both hands, it looks like a sandwich. We honk the horn and I shout something out the window. I don't remember exactly what I shouted, but I can imagine. Me at twenty years old, half my body hanging out of a moving vehicle, wind slapping my face and hair, hollering some smart-ass remark. *Get back to work!* Virgil looks up. I remember him looking up. He shouts some smart-ass comment back at me. *Get a job!* We laugh. I don't actually hear him laugh. I just see him. In the side-view mirror I see him. Shaking his head, watching us pull away.

It's Halloween night, 1994. Me, Alejandra, and David are dressed in drag. In this moment, Virgil and his wife are getting along, and he's staying with her at a condo on Shady Lane. They're having a party, friends are there, and booze is flowing. We walk up to his door, knock, and call out, "Trick or treat!" His wife answers and gets a kick out of our costumes and invites us in. Virgil is buzzed, not drunk yet, but getting there. He's happy to see us, gives us shit for our costumes, and introduces us to his friends. A few beers later, he hangs his arm over my shoulder, and in his loud booming voice, tells everyone at the party that I'm an artist and that I'm going to be famous someday. Everyone stares at me, strangers all of them, smiling and nodding. Virgil looks at me, glassy-eyed. His face grows serious. "When you become famous, cabrón, just don't forget me. And if you see me in the gutter, just throw me a bottle of wines!" Everyone busts up. But I know he means it. "Wines." That's not a typo, that's Virgil's speak. Plural. More than one. And throw it. Not hand it. Not even give it. Just throw it at me. In the gutter.

"Mijo . . . it's me . . ."
"Virgil?"
"Yeah . . . sorry to wake you . . ."
"It's okay . . . are you all right?"
"Can you come . . . come get me?"
"Right now?"
"Yeah . . . I'm . . . shit . . ."
"Where are you?"
"I'm at the bar . . ."
"Which one?"
"The Green Olive . . ."
"I'll be right there . . ."
"Wait . . . hold on . . ."
Muffled voices.
"Never mind, mijo . . . I got a . . . I can get a ride."
"Are you sure, tío? I'll come get you."
"No, no, no, no, no . . . I'll be home right now . . ."

23

TIME IS ALWAYS A FACTOR

January 29, 2018, California State Senate

WE ARE IN AN AMTRAK TRAIN barreling up the spine of the San Joaquin Valley. Outside the window a stream of greenish yellow streaks by. Winter closes early here, and the blossoms are already flirting their way onto branches. The rows of citrus and stone fruit are never-ending, only interrupted by the speckles of mostly brown bodies atop ladders, cutting away with precision what will end up on our tables. Moving in one direction or another has always fed my spirit. A woman once told me it was in my zodiac sign to be mobile. "Aquarians are notorious nomads," she said. This before she knew my history. Mobility is hardwired in my biological makeup. My father today drives diesels back and forth across the Southwest for a paycheck. Before that he was in the automobile business. And before that a migrant farmworker. My grandfather Felix and grandma Estela chased seasons their entire lives. They've lived in just about every state west of Oklahoma. Just as before them the Coahuiltecas, who we suspect were one of the original tribes our family descends from, traversed Mexico into the lower parts of Texas. Movement is in our blood. Something that took me years to understand. Whereas once I saw it as an impediment, I now know its purpose. And I teach this purpose to my children: *Everywhere you go is home.* I repeat this often.

But if there's one thing I've learned about modes of transportation, it's that trains are good for contemplating. Second only to driving.

Sacramento is our destination. The State Capitol.

Today marks the seventieth anniversary of the plane crash. We left Fresno early this morning and should be there by noon. With me are Jaime and Lilia Ramírez, Rosa María and her daughter Lisa, and, of course, Rumi and Salvador. At ages thirteen and nine they are my research assistants. Since Rumi was six and Sal was just two this is all they've ever known. Their story is now tied to these histories indefinitely. Sal was once held by Bea Franco during one of our many visits, while Rumi played with Bea's cat on the front porch. Since then, they have come with me to the crash site, have broken bread with many of the families, have watched me conduct interviews, have held cameras and audio equipment, and have seen me deliver this story to countless audiences. A while back I was speaking to a group of college students in San Antonio, and I caught Rumi silently mouthing every word that was coming out of my mouth, mocking me. I busted up laughing, and the audience couldn't figure out why. My children have memorized the routine and have taken some ownership over the work. At the release event for *All They Will Call You* I was signing books at the table and glanced over to find Salvador also signing books. And why not? These stories will be their inheritance.

About an hour into the trip Sal stands up in the aisle and something catches his eye. He whispers, "Dad, that man is reading your book." I discreetly turn to look, and a few rows back a man dressed in a suit is holding a copy of *All They Will Call You.* I recognize him. He's a young politician from Fresno. He catches me staring and doesn't hesitate to introduce himself. "You're the author," he says, pointing at the book. "Thank you for all the work you've done." He taps the book with his fingers. He knows we are heading to the State Capitol, and he knows why. But what he doesn't know is that in this train with me are families that represent three of the plane crash victims. I introduce him to them, and he's beside himself. "What an honor," he says. "This is unbelievable." By now Jaime and Lilia are well-versed in these discussions. But Rosa María and Lisa are new to it all. They reached out to me only a few months ago. And when a family is new to this it can be overwhelming. With time it'll get easier. With time we'll gather the stories of their relative, Francisco Durán Llamas, and will commit them to memory. But how much time this will all take is unknown. Months, years. This is the paradox.

⌾

When I spend time with a family, I am invited to the past. I live there for hours, sometimes days. Sometimes years. And then I return to the present. Back. Forth. Present and past. Time corrodes. Time's a giver. I've learned to "swim in the bittersweet." Wisdom from my therapist. I'm well aware that the stories are slipping into oblivion with the passing of each second. I arrive on the front porch of a family I have just found, and in the seconds it takes me to ring the doorbell, the Storykeeper I was here to speak with has passed. And with them go the stories. The families are too distraught to entertain my probing, and try as I might, I'm politely ushered away. In the weeks and months after, I'll reestablish contact with one or two family members, and they'll speak with me, but it's not the same. The magic of their story has lost its gravity. And there's no way to ever retrieve it. I know. I've tried.

This is why from the instant I meet a new family, I am already at work. It's a purposeful shift that has since become second nature. And one that I'm not necessarily proud of. At least not in the moment that it's happening. I feel like an earthworm, wriggling my way into the soil of their history, mining for nutrients unknown. I am gentle and deliberate. I try to be. The goal is to earn their trust. And more importantly, the trust of their elders. The oldest among them, inside whose hearts these stories are still very much alive. And it must be genuine. For permission to be had, the trust I seek must be used only for the purposes that I claim. Otherwise, there will be the dogs of karma to deal with. But regardless of my intention, I can never lose sight of the fact that with my arrival also comes the reopening of a wound. Not just any wound, but perhaps the hardest kind of wound to heal—a generational wound. A wound that's been passed on from mouth to ear to heart to head for more than seventy years. Difficult to heal because it's difficult to locate. Which is something that not all the families are prepared to deal with.

So the whole thing is a kind of spiritual courtship, and a balancing act. With each family I am confronting an accumulation of grief, but also the possibility of their collective closure. For this reason, when I first meet a new family, I try to remember to bring them an offering, and to let them know how honored I am to meet them. The offering typically consists of a packet. The contents may include documents and records concerning their relative who was killed, copies of the original newspapers of that time, recent articles showing the headstone and the location where their relative is buried, and a copy of *All They Will Call You.*

Next comes the frequency. How many times I visit or keep in touch with them over the months and years after is vital. I return with more offerings. Sometimes new information, sometimes an invitation. This is key. Leave them with more than you take. This is what don Miguel's horse story has taught me. But always I remain aware that time is quietly slipping away. People are aging as I write this. I am not exempt—

When I began this search in 2010, there wasn't a single white hair on my body, and wrinkles were few. Now there are too many of both to count. My daughter Rumi was just six years old at the time, and Salvador was two. Even so, Rumi was well aware by then that Dad "looks for people."

When she was still an infant, because we couldn't afford full-time day care, Rumi and I spent the majority of our days together. Often she'd fall asleep cradled in my left arm while I typed away with my right hand. The clacking of the keyboard her favorite lullaby. As she grew, I read poetry to her, and we often spoke of important matters, like why God made all the good-tasting foods bad for you and the bad-tasting foods good for you. We philosophized in our own way. I cultivated this type of closeness with Salvador too, but our circumstances had changed by then and time was harder to come by. I was working in Denver and commuting daily from Boulder, and our routine was dramatically different. By the time I got home we had dinner and then only two hours before the kids' bedtime. Still, making time for them was always my priority. We rode bikes, hiked the trails by our house, and played as much as possible. At bedtime I'd read them both a book, and then, once they were asleep, I'd head downstairs to the dining table to "find people." This usually kept me up past midnight, sometimes one or two in the morning, sometimes three. By now their mother and I were in our own quiet suffering. Arguments were frequent. The kids saw it all. We were robotically putting one foot in front of the other, like "good parents" do. We were getting older. So were they.

Back then, if someone had told me I'd still be searching for families thirteen years later, I would've thought them insane. But this is exactly what's happened. Thirteen passengers in thirteen years. At this rate, I'll be nearly seventy years old by the time I find everyone. Though in truth the search has been much more sporadic than that. It's been as messy and fragmented as the plane crash itself. The first book encompassed the seven families I had found up to then. That was supposed to be it. I was supposed to be done. But it was just the beginning. The door had opened, and more passengers would soon walk through. But there was one in particular whom I had been searching for since the very beginning, one that held my curiosity most. She was the only female among all the men. And she was reported to have been carrying baby clothes. I needed to know more. About the woman, and, if possible, the child.

24

THE UNEARTHING OF MARÍA RODRÍGUEZ SANTANA

Goodbye to my Juan, goodbye Rosalita,
adiós mis amigos, Jesús y María . . .

—WOODY GUTHRIE, "DEPORTEE (PLANE WRECK AT LOS GATOS)"

AMONG THE BODIES *of the Mexican nationals . . . was a woman with baby clothes beside her. No trace of a baby's body was found, however.*

This according to the *Coalinga Record.* Other newspapers added that the baby clothes were the color *blue.* The detail of the blue baby clothes haunted me. Something about an anonymous baby possibly killed on the banks of a creek beckoned me to dig deeper.

The woman was María Rodríguez Santana, and she was in fact the only Mexican female passenger on the flight. When I began my search in 2010, she was the first one I went looking for. I figured it would be easier to file through records of airplane deportations and locate one woman among the countless men. Especially since braceros were almost exclusively male. There was one clue that I held on to. It came from the Fresno-based Spanish-language independent newspaper *El Faro,* given to me by the Ramírez family. It was the only publication that printed all the names, hometowns, and last known addresses of the victims. In the list of names María's appears right after a passenger named Guadalupe Rodríguez, after which it reads, *esposa del anterior,* which translates to "wife of the former." The *Fresno Bee* also refers to her as Mrs. Rodríguez. By these accounts it appeared that the passengers María and Guadalupe Rodríguez were husband and wife, so I tried locating his family too, but my searches came up empty. I was intrigued by the possibility that a Mexican married couple had met their fate together, just as the pilot Frank Atkinson and his wife, the stewardess Bobbie Atkinson, had. And just as the Atkinsons were expecting, I was drawn to the possibility that María and Guadalupe were also with child, which would explain the blue baby clothes. Was I forcing a parallel for the sake of story? Was I compromising the search by clinging to my own ideas? Regardless, after two years I gave up on María, shuffled the tarot deck, and moved on to another name. Five years would pass. In early 2018, just days after I had been interviewed on National Public Radio's *Latino USA*, I received an email:

Hi Tim,

My name is Mike Rodriguez III, and I am a History / Ethnic Studies teacher in Santa Ana, California. María Rodríguez Santana was my grandfather's sister. Both were braceros who worked in San Jose and Fresno during the 1940s. My dad, also Mike Rodriguez, was born in San Jose, 7 months before his aunt's death.

My family would love to come out to Fresno to meet you and Jaime Ramírez, and thank you for putting up the tombstone for the people who died that day, including my tía. Growing up, I had always heard stories about the tía who died in the plane crash, but that was as far as it went. Her sister, my tía Eugenia, is still alive and lives in Watts, CA. I'm sure that she would love to hear from you.

I was looking through my Twitter account this morning when I saw the tweet from NPR Latino about your book and the interview. My jaw dropped to the floor. And it only took minutes and a few phone calls to realize that it was my tía. All of my family is very excited. And once again, thank you very, very much. I can't wait to read your book. Feel free to call me as well, and look forward to hearing from you.

ⓞ

I contacted Mike right away. Over the phone he told me that he'd come to learn of his aunt María from the stories told to him by his uncle Gonzalo, who lives in San Diego, just miles from El Centro, where the airplane was originally slated to land. If his story checked out, María would be the tenth passenger I had located.

Mike Rodriguez III: "Back in the '90s, when I was still a student at UC San Diego, I would feel homesick, so I'd visit my tío Gonzalo for conversations and get a home-cooked meal from my tía Rosa. I was nineteen, in college, you know, and my tío Gonzalo, he sorta took me under his wing. I'd go to their house and we'd have coffee and pan dulce, and my tía Rosa would make the best nopales I've ever had, and she'd make them just for me, and we'd eat and talk. We mostly talked about family, just catching up, stuff like that. At the time, I really didn't know a lot about my family, not the history. I met my grandpa Miguel, who was María's brother, just a few times, because he lived in Ensenada and I lived in Los Angeles, not too far away. But I didn't get to spend too much time around him. And my uncle Gonzalo, he's our family historian, he knows how everyone's connected, and it was he who first told me about my tía María and how she died in a plane crash. He didn't say too much about it at the time, not really, just that she was killed in an airplane. He never said she was being deported, or anything like that. So I didn't know anything about those details at the time. I just knew María was my grandpa Miguel's sister, and that she died in a plane crash in the forties. So when I heard your interview on NPR, I right away called my uncle Gonzalo to confirm the story, and that's when I was sure it was the same plane crash that my aunt María was killed in. That's when I sent you the email."

25

THE STORYKEEPER

HAVING DONE this work for more than a decade it's easy to spot who the Storykeeper of each family is. There's a certain fascination in their eyes when discussing this subject that isn't there in any of the other relatives, regardless of how close they were to the victim. At first, the Storykeeper might even act nonchalant, or suggest it's of mild interest to them, but they don't notice the subtleties, like how their body leans in toward the discussion whenever the subject is brought up, or how they carry their curiosity in their expression, or the rapt way they pay attention to the signs. The Storykeeper is a believer in signs. A believer in synchronicity. They're usually the one who will travel alone to seek the answers. And whether they acknowledge it or not, their investment is charged with something greater than the idea of the subject itself. The Storykeeper is the one who wants to know. Who *needs* to know. And for this reason, they remain steps ahead of the rest of the family when it comes to this subject. I've seen families designate one person to be the main point of contact for communication with me, but over time it's another relative, the Storykeeper, who ends up carrying out the work. And when a new piece of information is discovered, the Storykeeper is the one that the family looks to.

Initially, Mike Rodriguez III kept pointing me to his uncle Gonzalo, whom he called "the family historian." And while Gonzalo's memory is vital to the family's narrative, this particular story, this singular thread in the Rodriguez Santana family, is Mike's to bear. The signs are all there. It was he who discovered the story of my search. It was he who attended college in San Diego, where the plane was headed. Why else did he major in ethnic studies? Why else is it that he'd been teaching high-school students in Southern California about the injustices of historical erasure years before this story, or my name, would land on his radar? Despite how inclusive he tries to be, consulting his family at every turn, directing me to other relatives, it's he whom *they* have chosen. Or more accurately, it's he whom María has chosen. Mike Rodriguez III is the Storykeeper.

His is an average American story. Mike Rodriguez III was born in 1975 in Hollywood, California. He has a beautiful wife, Christina, and two children, Raymond and Maya, ages thirteen and nine. They live in a typical suburban home in Orange County, California. Every morning Mike wakes up, kisses Christina good morning, makes coffee, feeds their children cereal or sometimes treats them to donuts, and then drives them both to school. Shortly after, he arrives at his job teaching independent studies to students deemed "at risk." They are tenth through twelfth graders, many of whom have recently come from parts of Mexico and Central America. Mike's expertise is in U.S. history, world history, Latin American history, sociology, and ethnic studies. He earned his BA degree from UC San Diego, and his master's degree in education from UCLA. Sometimes his students refer to him as "Mr. Rodriguez," or sometimes "Mr. Ro Ro." He's at least six feet tall, walks with confidence, wears a moustache, and, on this particular morning, dons his signature blue Dodgers baseball cap. When first approaching you, from afar, he's a mountain. But as he gets closer you see the boyish grin on his face and discover that he's actually just a regular good guy.

Mike and I agreed to meet at Holy Cross Cemetery this morning. He's invited his aunt Bea, who is María's niece. They've driven the four hours from Los Angeles just to see the headstone and pay their respects. When we arrive, I walk them to the gravesite and express how I wish they'd found me just a few months sooner.

"Your family could've joined us at the California State Senate," I say. "It was a pretty special recognition ceremony for the seventieth anniversary of the crash."

"I wish we'd known," he replies.

As a historian himself, Mike understands that none of this process happens quickly. Before today, we had spent two months confirming that his family was in fact related to María. It's an awkward request. A complete stranger asking you to prove you are who you say you are. I explained to him that in order for me to write about the family, and to include their story in the larger archive of the plane crash at Los Gatos, it's a necessary step. I can't just take one's word for it. He gets it. Back in 2013, after the memorial headstone made international news, I was inundated with emails, people wondering if one of the passengers might be their lost relative. It's no surprise how many Mexicans have gone missing over the decades, never to be seen or heard from again. The Colibrí Center for Human Rights in Tucson, Arizona, reports that right now there are more than 3,500 missing persons, Mexicanos, lost in the desert. And families will go to great lengths to locate their loved ones, even after decades. I was exhausted by fielding all the inquiries, and worried that my empathy would fade. Plus, I had learned from working on Bea Franco's story that people will go around writing narratives about others without having done the work. I was grateful that Mike understood this, and that his family was willing to help me search for documents that would confirm their relation to María. We were establishing trust.

ꩰ

Mike and Bea stand over the headstone in silence for a few minutes. Bea places flowers down on the grave. More silence. Mike tells me that he read my book.

"That's great," I say. "I'm honored."

"I found an error," he says, adjusting his glasses. "Our aunt María wasn't married."

It catches me off guard. "What do you mean?"

"You wrote in your book that the passenger María was married. But she wasn't."

"Are you sure?"

"Yeah, we're sure." He looks at Bea. "We would've definitely known. She was here in the United States with her brother Miguel, my grandpa, and they were close. If she was married he would've definitely known, and so would the whole family."

"The newspaper *El Faro* says she's the wife of one of the passengers," I explain.

"Yeah, that paper's wrong. Everyone in my family knows she wasn't married."

"Do you know if she had a baby?"

"No, she definitely didn't have a baby."

"Are you sure?"

"Yeah, I'm sure."

Silence. "Shit, I apologize," I say.

The news of this doesn't sit well with me. What I wrote about María in *All They Will Call You* is inaccurate. It's a hard pill to swallow. I will need to revise myself.

Mike glances down at the headstone.

He and Bea talk about their tía Eugenia. Their wish is to bring her here one day, to see where her sister María is buried. They say her memory is vivid.

"Do you think I could speak with your tía Eugenia at some point?" I ask.

Mike looks to his aunt.

"I think so. We'd have to check with the family, but I think that's a good idea," Bea says.

He adds, "My tía is up there in age, so our family is kinda protective of her."

"I understand." I want to put them at ease. "We can do it however your family feels comfortable. Even if it's just for a few minutes."

As much as I try and hide it, Mike senses my urgency. I've seen too many almost testimonies slip away. Time is relentless. I'm prepared to do whatever it takes to get a chance to speak with Eugenia. In fact, it doesn't even necessitate speaking. To just sit in her presence would be enough. They assure me they'll try and make it happen. I give them the phone numbers of some of the other families, especially the ones I've been working with for years now, the Ramírez family, so that they can call and see for themselves that I'm trustworthy. Later, Mike will tell me that he did call the other families, and that it was helpful. Our visit is short, and I answer as many questions as they throw at me. And then I leave them there, at the gravesite, for a moment of privacy with their aunt María.

26

MARÍA IN THE UNITED STATES

UNTIL MIKE Rodriguez III contacted me about the possibility of interviewing his tía Eugenia, María's story would be conveyed to me only by the collective memory of her relatives, none of whom knew her personally, but all of whom had been told the stories.

Naturally, there are many contradictions, as well as things agreed upon by all. For instance, they all agree that the only reason María had come to the United States in the first place was to be with her brother Miguel. They had a special bond, and when he told her about the opportunities in California, she trusted him and made the trek. How exactly she crossed into the United States nobody knows. But it's also generally agreed that the plan included living in the Bay Area and working, and sending money back home to their parents Hilario and Antonia in Ensenada. Beyond this is where the contradictions begin:

"María lived with her siblings in Fresno for a short while—"

"María worked with her brother Miguel at a restaurant in San Jose—"

"I remember she worked with her sister Micaela picking green beans near San Jose—"

"They were picking beans for Libby's cannery in Sunnyvale—"

"Probably before she moved to San Francisco with Miguel and his girlfriend Mary Rios—"

"No, it was later that Miguel and Mary Rios joined them—"
"Yes, that's right—"
"Or was it the other way around?—"

This is how all of our remembered histories work. But the accuracy of these details isn't important to those who share María's blood. What is important, and perhaps all that really mattered, back then as much as now, is that sometime between 1947 and 1948, María and her siblings had come to the United States to seize all the opportunities they could. Impossible to imagine how this single decision would forever change the trajectory of their family's lives.

In the mid-1940s, Antonia and her husband Hilario reluctantly left their ranchito in San José del Refugio, in the state of Jalisco, to move north to the frontera town of Tijuana. The plan was to find work and start a new chapter.

Mike Rodriguez II: "My grandmother Antonia Santana was part of a huge clan in Jalisco, and she had a brother, Tomás, who moved to Tijuana years before. He made candies and sold them to the stores around there, and parts of Baja. The way I understand it, it was my tío Tomás who talked my grandmother Antonia into moving to Tijuana. She already had the kids, and María was one of them, the second eldest. It was Felícitas, María, Miguel, Micaela, Guadalupe, Eugenia, and Isabel, in that order."

Gonzalo: "You see, Felícitas was already in Ensenada. She'd come to Baja with her husband because the Mexican government was afraid that the Japanese would come to Baja, so they wanted to populate it. In the 1940s lots of land in Baja was being given away, so my grandma was able to secure property around 1947. They arrived on December 25, 1946, and my mother remembers working for two weeks, and that's when they secured a lot."

Mike Rodriguez II: "My grandmother loved Ensenada, so they packed up and left Tijuana. We weren't poor, or rich, but we were in good shape there. My grandfather Hilario was a good worker, illiterate but worked hard, knew how to make houses, stuff like that. From what I understand, María didn't live in Ensenada very long. She left for the United States shortly after the family arrived there."

Gonzalo: "Her brother Miguel had already been in the United States prior to 1946, because he had sent money home. He even sent a letter back to Jalisco saying, 'We won the war.' So that means he would've been in the United States prior to 1945. The money he sent helped them move to Ensenada in December of 1946, so he was in the United States before that. Which means María would've arrived in the United States around 1947."

From here the stories are weathered by time. But there are a few agreed-on facts. At one point Miguel did work at a restaurant in San Jose, and María, Eugenia, and Micaela all ended up working there too. Their sister Felícitas did stay in Ensenada, and she was married to a Mexican soldier. It was they who had the family's firstborn child. However, due to the demands of the military, their child would not be as close to his aunts and uncles as some of the children who were to come later.

While in California Miguel would fall in love with Mary Rios, and in San Jose they'd have their first child, Michael Rodriguez II, according to his birth certificate (though today he is known as Mike Sr.). But given the uncertainty of their circumstances, caring for the baby would be difficult, so at just a few months old he was sent to Ensenada to be raised by his grandmother Antonia.

Mike Rodriguez II: "I was the luckiest guy in the world to be raised by my grandmother. I was spoiled rotten. There was nothing she wouldn't give me. Growing up there, so close to the beach in Ensenada, we would get up at five a.m. and go fish. And on our way back home we would buy a stack of newspapers and sell them to people in the streets. Not that we had to, it was just for fun mostly. But I've worked since I was seven years old. I would help stock the store, or tear up boxes, or go run errands for my grandmother. And even though I was technically the second child born into the family, I was really the one who was closest to all of my uncles and aunts, and my tía María loved me very much." He pauses. Tears gather behind his glasses. He wipes them away with his finger. Takes a few seconds to collect himself before he continues. "When she was killed . . . well, I was around seven months old at the time. And I was the child closest to María, and probably the only one of us she really knew. Like I said, I was living in Ensenada, where she was returning to. And she had just been with my dad Miguel and my birth mother Mary Rios in San Jose, and they knew María was coming to see me." He pauses once more. Chokes back tears. "The blue baby clothes María was carrying were for me. And when I learned that . . . that she had been carrying clothes for me, it was . . . I mean . . . she was bringing that for *me*."

There is another story that resonates.

It takes place during a window of time that I hope to ask Eugenia about, because it happened in San Francisco. And the San Francisco immigration office is also where the deportation of the passengers was ordered. It is an idyllic memory that offers us a glimpse of a María filled with life and optimism.

Gonzalo: "My mother Micaela told us that when they were in San Francisco they would cross the bay in my uncle Miguel's car. They had to put the car in the ferry, you see. It would be my mom, María, my uncle Miguel, and his girlfriend Mary Rios. And I guess Mary said, 'I'm not gonna ride on that thing.' And my uncle said, 'What do you mean you're not? It's already moving.' And they all started laughing. They always crossed from San Francisco to Richmond like that. And my mom told me that María used to really like that ferry ride."

It's easy for the mind to want to hold on to a single lasting image of our loved ones painted in light. Sometimes our survival depends on it. The image of María and her siblings crossing the bay by ferry. The perfume of the ocean. Seagulls squawking overhead. The frigid water lapping against the ferry as the late-afternoon sun sinks down beyond the skyline, silhouetting the bridge that connects the East Bay to the city. By now, the war almost two years gone. It must've felt like a little bit of serenity in the madness of the world. In a moment like this it would be impossible for María to imagine that in a few months' time she would be crossing the same bridge in a bus filled with Mexicans en route to the Oakland Municipal Airport for deportation. But the signs are always there. Left only for the families to decipher.

Gonzalo: "My mother said that when María was leaving back to Ensenada she told her, 'You can have all my clothes, in case I don't come back.' That's exactly what she said to her. And after she died, my mother realized it was an omen. She believed that María must've felt something was going to happen to her."

Memories disintegrate. They always do. When this happens, I see it as an invitation to take a step back, ponder other possibilities of the story I think I'm after. María's story. What am I not paying attention to? Where am I not looking? I reconsider the message. Who is María without the people who populated her world? Perhaps it's less about who María was in 1948, and more about where she exists today—in whom she exists.

I reach out to Mike Rodriguez III and leave him a message. It's been three months now since he first said he'd arrange for me to meet with his aunt Eugenia. Finally the call arrives.

He tells me that he spoke with the family and says they'd all feel more comfortable with me if I send the questions I plan to ask Eugenia in advance. He reminds me that this is a touchy subject for his aunt, and that the family is being protective for her sake. I tell him I understand, and I email my questions. I don't hear back for another few weeks.

When he finally does call, he's excited to tell me that the family will be gathering to speak with Eugenia about the incident, and about her sister María.

"We want to make it a kind of weekend celebration of her life," he says.

I tell him that's a beautiful idea, and I'm excited about the opportunity. He breaks the news.

"But we decided that it should just be family."

I can't think of a response quickly enough.

"I'm really sorry about this," he says. "I hope you understand."

Silence.

It's easy for me to forget who this story belongs to. Sometimes I get so caught up in believing I have the right to it just because this search has consumed the last thirteen years of my life. What can I say? I remind myself that it's not *my story*. Nor is it my family. I check my entitlement at the door. "Of course I understand," I say. But my brain won't give up. It wants to find a way. "What if I don't ask any questions at all?" I say to Mike. "What if I just sit there quietly and observe? You won't even know I'm there."

He hesitates. "I'm sorry, man."

I'm left thinking. From the perspective of the family, I get it. From the perspective of history, there has to be a way. We have to document Eugenia's testimony. It comes to me.

"Can I ask you for a favor? When you do talk with your tía Eugenia, and if you do get to ask her questions about María, can you please record that conversation on video? You don't have to share it with me, but just so that your family has it, and keeps it?"

"Oh, I definitely plan to record it. I'll be documenting the whole thing."

And this is why Mike Rodriguez III is the Storykeeper.

27

SEMBLANCE OF CLOSURE

A FEW WEEKS LATER Mike III calls to tell me how it all went. "We finally had the family gathering. We sat down with my tía Eugenia to talk about María. I'm so glad we did that too. She said she felt appreciated, you know, that we all just sat and listened to her story."

He's hesitant to share more with me in this moment, but I don't pry. I want to ask questions, but it's not the right time. He continues, "I guess my only regret, if you can call it that, is that I wish my grandma, my tía Chavela, and my tía Micaela were alive, so we could take them and my tía Eugenia to the grave to honor their sister María's life as well. They all held a lot of pain. A lot of pain. That's why my great-grandmother Antonia didn't want anyone talking about it. And none of them did. I mean not until just recently. Until we sat down with my tía Eugenia." I can tell he feels good about what his family has accomplished. They have initiated their own closure. And this is the whole point, after all. I tell him I'm happy to hear it. Grateful that he's willing to share the update with me. We agree to touch base again soon.

൭

On Saturday, August 18, 2018, Mike III calls to tell me that his aunt Eugenia has passed away. He's silent for a moment.

"I'm so sorry," I say.

"She was surrounded by the love of her family," he tells me. He reminds me that she was the last matriarch of that generation to go. "They're all gone now," he adds, struggling to hear himself admit it.

Eugenia R. Andrade died at age 89, in South Gate, Los Angeles, California. She was the last sister of passenger María Rodríguez Santana. The last person alive who had ever physically touched her. And I never had the privilege of meeting her.

Four Years Later

"I'm so sorry that you weren't able to speak to my mom before she passed," Eugenia's daughter, Sandra Andrade, writes to me in an email. "Although we're very protective of our family's history, I know there were many stories that she would've loved to share."

Time has a way of coaxing a story back into the light. I can't help but see Sandra's words as an invitation. If I proceed cautiously, with care and consideration, the story might allow me to gather it. John Steinbeck once wrote that some stories are like certain sea creatures, in that they are "so delicate they break and tatter under the touch." And the only way to gather them is to let them "ooze and crawl of their own will onto your knife blade." And he's right. So I lower my blade down into the water and wait. There are people willing to take further measures just to "get the story," I know. Certain journalists, perhaps, or even writers relentlessly pursuing a good thread. But after having been on this journey for thirteen years, I find myself retreating back to the belief that, at the end of the day, the only story I am truly after is the one that offers itself to me. The story that consents to this exchange. Which is to say, the story that is after me. In this case, María is the one who decides what I need to hear and not hear. My only job is to pay attention. Sandra's email continues:

> *I asked my mother if she could make a statement of who my aunt María was and here's what she said: "María was a strong woman and I looked up to her. She was a hard worker that never let her personal circumstances be an excuse for not working. She loved us very much and was*

always very giving and generous. She was an extremely independent woman, and that was something frowned upon at that time. I guess you can say she was audacious. Sadly, I wasn't able to spend as much time with her as I would have liked, but I never forgot my sister María, and I still include her in my daily prayers."

María Rodríguez Santana, circa 1947.

28

MR. RO RO, AN AMERICAN SCHOOL TEACHER

"I THINK ABOUT MY TÍA MARÍA a lot these days. About what she and my grandpa Miguel, and all their siblings, went through just to get us all here. But thanks to them, we're now in this position. I was born in this country, and my dad was born here. I mean, I was here when the Rodney King riots happened. That was part of my reality, talk about American, you know? Stuff like that shaped who I am. I remember about a week after the riots, my school, Loyola High School, was finally letting students return to class. And I'll never forget driving my Ford Escort down Venice Boulevard and just seeing all the damage, you know. I'd seen it all on TV and for the first time in my life I remember thinking, What would make a person so angry that they'd burn down their own neighborhood? I think I was just trying to understand where it was coming from. At that time I didn't really understand inequality, or even racism really. I mean, not like my dad did. He was caught in the Watts riots, and he'd always tell us that story, about when he was a teenager and was working at the Chorizo Factory on 111th right in the middle of where the riots broke out. He knew what that anger looked like, and he knew why. And here I was, thirty years later, and I'm experiencing this for myself. I remember all the buildings burnt down, and just feeling like there was just so much rage in that. And I was just seventeen, and I guess that's really where it all started for me. I mean, it wasn't just black folks upset. There were immigrant mothers too, getting boxes of diapers from stores. I mean, just all that extreme poverty was exposed to me, and for the first time I was seeing it with my own eyes. And I think that's when things started to make sense to me. I remember once hanging out with some friends in Westchester, a suburb we called Whitechester, and me and some friends went to a party there, and it was night, of course, and we were the only people of color there. The cops rolled up and everyone scattered, but we were the ones who got stopped and frisked. They searched my car, didn't find anything, so they let us go. It wasn't until later that I looked back and realized what that meant, or how moments like that shaped me.

"And now here I am, an inner-city educator, helping my students with immigrant rights, keeping ICE from taking their families away. Students have literally cried in my arms, telling me stories about how they crossed, or how they don't want ICE to deport their parents. I had one student, her name was Cielo, she was in my People's History of Orange County class, and her dad was picked up right in front of their home by ICE. They swarmed in and got him one morning. It happened quick. They showed up out of nowhere, and when he realized what was happening he told his son to run inside and get the family, but by the time they all came outside he was gone. Just like that. Cielo was strong, she never broke down. Not in front of me, at least. But it was heartbreaking to see that. You feel helpless. She asked me for advice, for help. She and her older sister took on the responsibility of the house. I'm sure it was hard on them. They wanted to stay under the radar. Some lawyers did pro bono work for them to help their case. We all started to advocate for their dad's release process. I took a trip with another teacher, my good friend Linn, to the Adelanto Detention Center to testify for him at the hearing. The immigration court there is a little room, like a private detention center. We were all there supporting Cielo and her family. Maybe a month or two later they finally released him. His case is still pending, I believe. Cielo ended up getting accepted to Harvard, and now she's there studying medicine.

"Teaching in a migrant community, I've learned just as much about resiliency from my students as I have taught them. I've seen this resiliency within my dad's family too, as well as migrants from Mexico who have raised children in a country where the powerful haven't always seen us as equals, or viewed us as people that have contributed to this society. My dad said something to me once that has always stayed with me: 'Always strive to make the next generation better than you.' This is what I try and do with my own kids, and for my students. I want them to strive to make the world better, and sustainable for the next seven generations, which is based on an Iroquois philosophy. I want to empower my students with knowledge that'll uplift their communities. I want them to know that they're valued, they are central to our country, and they're going to do great things in the future."

29

ENTERING MEXICO (A PSYCHOLOGICAL PRIMER)

THE DECISION to pursue my search for families in Mexico didn't come easy. In fact, it was the aspect that I'd dreaded the most. I had never been to the internal parts of Mexico, or, as my friends referred to it, the *real* Mexico. I had only ever been to the frontera, places like Tijuana, Palomas, and Juárez. According to my friends, the two were completely different realities. Of course, I had no way of knowing any of this. I only knew that my family, on both my maternal and paternal sides, had lost all contact with that part of our past. For four generations, the Zuñigas and Hernandezes had been born on the northern side of the border, and in some cases only a few feet away from the line, but enough to make them U.S. citizens. My grandmother Magdalena was from Columbus, New Mexico, where Pancho Villa famously fought against the 13th Cavalry. My great-grandparents Manuel and Nicolasa were said to have been caught in the middle of that incident. Our lore is here, rooted in this desert. The adobe remnants of my great-grandparents' home can still be found on Road 11. I've lifted shards of their DNA from underneath the chaparral that stands guard over this place.

And yet, regardless of how close we were to that line in the dirt, it was made clear to me very early on by my parents that we were not from Mexico. *They* were from Mexico. Because *they* had customs and a reality much different from ours. *Theirs* was a poor country of mostly rural folks. We had toilets and running water. *Their* children worked the streets at an early age. We had microwaves and fast food. *They* spoke Spanish. We spoke some bastardized version of it, and only when necessary.

English was our primary tongue. My parents listened to music in English, watched television shows in English, and played American radio. The only Spanish we'd get came from Tex-Mex music in which the two languages were stitched beautifully together by accordion riffs, and only on weekends or barbecues. Like all Tejanos, my dad was proud of being from the Lone Star State and never hesitated to brag about its traditions and history. Meanwhile, my mom constantly reminded my sister and me that we were also from New Mexico—a complex mix of indigenous blood and Spanish temperament, never choosing one over the other, but recognizing that each has its place within us. The same way that when we are asked if we prefer red or green chile we will sometimes say, "Christmas." It isn't a choice at all; it's who we are, all of it, for better or worse.

And this was what I saw around my house as a kid. Growing up in central California we were the only family on our block that hung the Texas flag over our garage and dangled sunburnt ristras from our front porch. It wasn't until I was an adult that I realized not everyone eats their enchiladas with a fried egg on top, and when I went to school with my Dallas Cowboys jacket on I didn't know I'd come home with a busted lip for it.

It was a matter of survival. My grandma Estela often told me stories of how she was physically attacked for being brown, pummeled with rocks by white boys, while growing up in Corpus Christi, Texas. For reasons like this, my grandparents made it clear to their children, "The next time a teacher cracks your knuckles with a ruler for speaking Spanish, you look that teacher in the eye and tell her, 'My dad fought in World War II and the Korean War.' You tell her, 'I'm just as American as you.'"

But even being armed with their parents' affirmation of Americanness didn't protect my mom and dad from having the Mexicanness beat out of them. The next day at school, they'd let a Spanish word slip, and right there, in front of the class, they would get hit with rulers. Public education circa 1950s. A seed was planted. Spanish became a liability. Instead, my parents would teach their children, not only to learn, but to master the language of the oppressor. They would name their firstborn Timothy, but they would call him Timmy. What name more American-sounding, which is to say more white-sounding, which is to say more safe-sounding, than Timmy—that beloved 1950s television blond kid with his trusty dog Lassie?

And this is how we arrive at the source of why my Spanish is, as one might call it, compromised. It wasn't merely *not* taught to me. Since before the womb I was already being groomed to master the Master's tongue. Spanish was the inheritance of trauma. Just ask the tribes who were the original peoples of modern-day Mexico if this isn't true. When Spanish arrived on the shores of Veracruz its accent mark was a thorn that yielded a generational curse that has never been broken. No matter how you slice it, Spanish bears bloodshed across time and geography, regardless of whether you speak it or don't. It's only a question of how close in proximity you are to it, and where you find yourself standing. In my family's case, growing up in the post-WWII Southwest, speaking Spanish was the impediment. Ironically, it was the language my parents turned to whenever they'd argue. As if, subconsciously, hurting one another in the tongue associated with the most pain just made sense.

English was our future. And so we shape-shifted. My skills were impeccable from day one. By second grade I was receiving awards in valley-wide poetry recitation contests. By third grade I had memorized Langston Hughes's poems. By fourth grade I knew all the lyrics to "The Message" by Grandmaster Flash and the Furious Five: *It's like a jungle sometimes it makes me wonder how I keep from goin' under.* So did all the other brown kids I grew up with who called the fields of the Central Valley home. Many of us already three or four generations removed from Mexico.

It was only once I became an adult and was expected to account for myself in adult circles that my limited Spanish became a source of shame. Don't even try and utter a sentence if you aren't absolutely sure you got it down, or you'll be laughed out of your own skin and flagellated by the gatekeepers of brownness. I learned this lesson the hard way. To this day, Spanish-speaking elders will still publicly shame those of us who "perdieron su lengua." But make no mistake, our tongue was never "lost." It was stripped from us. First on the shores of the Motherland, and then again in the classrooms of the Otherland. And do you know how much strength it takes to walk yourself back through that generational corridor of shame? How much time? This was the internal crisis I found myself in when I even imagined I could somehow enter Mexico, knock on the doors of complete strangers, and start probing the intimate matters of their lives, as if I had any right.

Thank God for my grandma Estela.

It was because of her that I learned to understand Spanish. In the same way one comes to discard one's language for the sake of survival, it's also for the sake of survival that one comes to learn it. Whenever she would take care of me, which was often, there was an unspoken agreement between my grandma and me. The deal was, I could speak to her in English and she would speak to me in Spanish, and like this, in the most nonjudgmental exchange, we'd learn the other language. And we did learn, but only how to listen for it, how to hear it. We never required the other to speak it. In this way, she allowed me to exist without ever having to feel ashamed. And perhaps I did the same for her. Perhaps we were holding hands and taking steps back through that corridor of shame together in some small way. Perhaps, without our knowing it, we were healing each other. Because of her I learned how to decode Spanish. How to read the inflections, tone, context of the situation, and physical gestures. It began to make sense to me. It was through these exchanges with my grandma Estela that my confidence grew.

I became an expert listener of Spanish. Little did I know that it would be one of the greatest tools I had when searching for families in Mexico—the ability to listen and discern what was being said, and yet not feel compelled to interrupt the dialogue. A peculiar trait, but extremely valuable. I was a perfect witness. Nothing more than a pair of ears and eyes, a sensorial recording machine. I could focus solely on receiving information. Which is to say, I could focus on being wholly present, in the moment. Not in the fictitious future, or in the remembered past, but in the here and now. I began to understand what the journalist Gay Talese once said about language barriers: "What people say isn't necessarily what they believe. My reporting is less about talking to people than what I call the fine art of hanging out."

Once I had exhausted every avenue of research from behind my cozy desk in the States, I knew it was time to face what I had been putting off since the beginning. Mexico was calling. There was no way around it. I'd have to step into the corridor. But this time without the gentle hand of my grandma Estela to guide me. At least not in physical form. Alone, I would be made to confront the layers of conditioning and shame that had accumulated in my family over generations.

A week before I was set to leave, in a moment of panic, I considered coming up with a good excuse to cancel my trip, but I knew it would be a cop-out. If I was serious about this search, this was the next step. It was the only step. My relatives didn't make it any easier.

"Do you really need to go there?"

I assured them that I did.

"But Mexico's not safe. Have you seen the news?"

I knew they were referring to the forty-three students from the Ayotzinapa Rural Teachers' College who had recently been abducted and disappeared.

"Imagine what we look like to other countries. Our schoolchildren are gunned down, and our government looks the other way. What's worse?" It was my only rebuttal.

They understood but were still worried for me.

I was sure. They were not.

"Well, if you need to go, then just be smart about it. It's Mexico. Their laws are different. Not like here. Do you have people there to help you? How will you get around? Will you have a translator?"

In their words I could hear the concerns of my grandparents, all of them, Alejandro and Magdalena, Felix and Estela, reinforcing the idea that Mexicanos were just a different breed of people from us. I realized then it would be easier to walk the corridor without the added weight of their baggage. I had to leave their past behind me. Besides, I was confident about one thing. One thing my family did not know. I was in conversation with *them.* And *they* would be there to walk with me. I trusted this. With all of me. I trusted them. And I went.

30

DISEMBODIMENT

Being invisible and without substance,
a disembodied voice, as it were, what else
could I do? What else but to try and tell
you what was really happening when your
eyes were looking through?

—RALPH ELLISON, *INVISIBLE MAN*

August 3, 2019, El Paso, Texas

AT 10:15 a.m., a twenty-one-year-old terrorist named posts a 2,356-word manifesto on the internet, outlining his justification for the act he plans to commit within the next six minutes. He writes: *This attack is a response to the Hispanic invasion of Texas*... He's driven eleven hours from his home in Allen, Texas, all the way to El Paso, my home. He's aware that our city of almost 800,000 residents is approximately 80 percent "Hispanic." He's done his homework. At around 10:21 a.m. he walks into the Cielo Vista Walmart on the east side of town carrying a semiautomatic rifle and opens fire on families who are there to buy school supplies for their children. Employees hear gunshots and see people running. They hurry and direct people to the back doors. But the terrorist is now walking around the store blasting round after round, and he does not stop. Eyewitness accounts tell us that *a man and his aging mother ducked between toy machines to hide. A child was left alone but then was quickly rescued by a stranger before the man started shooting at him. An old man shielded his family but then was instantly shot and killed.* In minutes blood is splattered on the floors and between the aisles. The terrorist strolls slowly through the store, picking off victims randomly for ten to fifteen minutes. After which he returns to his car and drives away. Minutes later he's captured "without incident" and arrested. In all, the terrorist has killed twenty-three people and wounded twenty-four others. I receive a text:

Active shooter in El Paso happening right now!

Are you and the kids okay?

It's from my mom. I respond by telling her that we haven't arrived in El Paso yet. We're still en route. We had left California early that morning and were driving home as it was happening. We arrive that evening and, not owning a television, the kids and I sit on our couch and check the internet for updates.

"It happened at the Walmart near the Cinemark Theater," Rumi says, "on the east side." We live on the west side of El Paso, but we're familiar with the area because it's near the reptile shop where we get supplies for Salvador's bearded dragon.

ᘓ

The next morning, I decide we need to get away from the news and out of our heads. The streets are sparse and quiet. Everywhere we go people are solemn. At the gas station. At the park. The overall mood reminds me a lot of what it felt like in the days after the September 11 terrorist attacks. A collective grief hangs in the air. El Paso is in shock.

The next two days we mostly stay home. We're in a new house and so we focus on settling in. But there comes a point where we need groceries and other products, and so it makes sense that we should go to Walmart, which is just two blocks from our house.

As we approach the parking lot, I can sense Rumi's apprehension. We've managed to avoid the discussion, but now we are faced with it. She admits that it's all taking a toll on her. She's "afraid of what could happen next."

I remind her that El Paso has consistently been ranked among the top three safest cities in America. A statistic that we've touted for all the years we've lived here.

"It doesn't feel that way anymore," she says.

"Going into Walmart is part of the healing," I offer. "Even though it's not the same Walmart where it happened." She doesn't buy it. "We can't let fear determine how we live our lives."

She rolls her eyes.

We are greeted at the entrance by armed security guards and two police officers. The tension is palpable. The place is quiet, almost completely empty; shoppers are scarce. The few who are there keep to themselves. The emptiness only makes it that much harder to distract oneself. In the silence, my mind invents a story. I am reimagining the incident as I walk the aisles. People scrambling for their lives. Gunshots. How would I have reacted? Blood. What would I have done? I like to think I would've done anything to protect my children. I like to think others would've done anything to protect us. And I believe they would have. I believe in the basic goodness of people. I need to believe in this, otherwise I'll walk around the world paranoid. I refuse to be a prisoner of my own time. I have to get out of my head. We push our cart around a corner and find ourselves in front of a white couple wearing shirts that read *El Paso Strong* and *Amor Para El Paso.* And it brings me some sense of relief. The word *Amor.* What the presence of that word alone can do for you in just the right moment, under the right circumstances.

"Where'd you get your shirts?" I ask them.

They're surprised by my question. We talk for several minutes. Later I will not recall what about. But I know it wasn't about the shooting. Maybe it was about the weather. The heat is unbearable these days. The monsoons offer no solace. In this moment, everything we say sounds like a metaphor. What I pay attention to most is the essence of our exchange. We are mutually looking for reasons to communicate with one another. Strangers in our city, reaching out to remind ourselves there's still kindness in the world. It's a brief but necessary exchange. And I can see that it lifts Rumi's spirits. They even shake our hands as we leave. Any excuse to touch.

ᘓ

May 9, 2019

It is three months before the Walmart shooting. President Trump speaks at a rally in Panama City Beach, Florida. In response to thousands of Central American families who are trekking to the U.S. border to seek safety and asylum, he says: *I mean when you have fifteen thousand people marching up, and you have hundreds and hundreds of people, and you have two or three border security people that are brave and great . . . and don't forget . . . we can't let them use weapons, we can't. Other countries do. We can't. I would never do that. But how do you stop these people?*

Woman from the crowd: *Shoot 'em!*

The crowd cheers.

President Trump (laughing): *That's only in the Panhandle you can get away with that . . .*

The crowd erupts in applause.

Trump pauses for comedic effect, tugs his lapel, smirks, repeats: *Only in the Panhandle!*

The crowd roars with laughter and cheers.

꩜

Florida is a panhandle state.
So is Texas.

꩜

In Texas, the years between 1910 and 1920 were known as La Matanza, or sometimes the Hour of Blood. It was a decade-long, state-sanctioned era of ethnic cleansing, in which the Texas Rangers lynched, dragged, shot, and killed over five thousand brown-skinned people and buried them in mass unmarked graves. It was open season. Brown families lived in constant fear of white men mounted on horses wielding rifles with the authority of a badge. Some historians may take issue that I am not specifying "Mexicans" here. But let's get this straight: a brown body was a brown body, nationality be damned. Still other historians will argue over the numbers and the years, but that's only because the records have been mostly redacted on this dark chapter, blacked out, burned, or disappeared. Besides, the exact number isn't the issue. One is too many.

ↄ

A panhandle is not the hottest part of the pan. The hottest part is where the pan kisses the flame. This is where my children and I live.

ↄ

Although his manifesto says "Hispanics," the Walmart terrorist does not actually mean Hispanics. Let me clarify. His mission is specifically to shoot a group of people whose skin pigmentation is darker than white. How much darker? He will decide. When he enters the store he will not be requiring documents for proof of race, citizenship, or nationality. He will walk in with one goal and one goal only—to seek out brown bodies and "shoot 'em" indiscriminately. This is what hate does. It has no order. Hate claims to have a target and a rationale, but it makes no promises. If amid the terror one person should step forward and declare, "I'm not Hispanic, I'm white!" I assure you this will not be enough. Your ethnicity will not spare you from hate. In fact, it was not enough. Not that day in that Walmart. Because it did not spare a grandmother named Margie Reckard, or a beloved uncle named David Johnson. Nor did it spare a victim named Alexander Gerhard Hoffman Roth, who was actually born in Germany. And what is racism if not hate justified by an idea? Racism spares no one. Don't be fooled, racism has no loyalties, except to the idea. Not even the racist himself is exempt. Especially not the racist. This is why he or she or they will inevitably die for the idea.

ↄ

In the months following, the Cielo Vista Walmart was shut down and a chain link fence was lassoed around the perimeter. Large green tarps were draped over it, blocking the view of the scene. A redaction on a grand scale. But this city is no stranger to walls. We know what's on the other side. Spontaneously, people turned the fence into a memorial site. Not unlike others we've seen in cities across the country: Dayton, Gilroy, Boulder, Buffalo. The list grows.

The store itself was renovated. The interior scrubbed, gutted, and reshaped. If it looks like a different store, customers will return. Sales will continue. As a gesture of empathy, the corporate giant would hire an architecture firm from Arkansas to design a more permanent memorial. A bronze-colored cylinder made of aluminum, which stands thirty feet tall and lights up at night, is what they came up with. They call it the Grand Candela. Big Candle. It stands, out of the way, in a parking lot that overlooks Interstate 10. Unless you know exactly where to look, it's an unnoticeable structure, with no gravity. Perhaps it was designed with this in mind. A memorial that does not draw attention to itself. It may as well have been named the Grand Pacifier. As far as memorials go, it's a lackluster gesture to recognize what has come to be known as "the deadliest attack on Latinos in modern U.S. history." Pay attention to memorials. Some serve to never let us forget. Others serve simply so that those in power can sleep at night. In which case, the incident itself becomes a footnote in the margins of our collective memory.

November 4, 2019

Three months after the Walmart massacre, El Paso is still tender. The wound slow to heal. But at least we've managed to stop holding our breath. Our children have finally begun settling back into school. The El Paso Independent School District assures us it has implemented further safety measures. So safe that it won't even share with us parents what those measures are. Police officers guard the schools, as well as the entrances of all Walmarts. Rumi is once again thriving at Franklin High. The days are calm. We don't forget. But we do go about our lives. It's always there. Some days less so. Some days we feel normal again. Like today. Today feels like another regular Monday. But then two texts appear, minutes apart:

> Franklin, Polk, and Guerrero on lockdown until further notice. Police incident in neighborhood. No person in or out until further notice.
>
> Txt STOP to cancel

> Franklin, Guerrero, and Polk upgraded to lockout. Instruction will continue as normal on campus, but no person will be allowed in or out.
>
> Txt STOP to cancel

~~We are scared.~~ I am scared.
~~We live in constant~~ I live in constant fear.
We don't know what'll come next, or from where.
~~We~~ I only know that it will come.
I'm aware that I'm a brown man in America. ~~I'm aware.~~ We are aware.
And I'm aware that I've ~~historically~~ been ~~erased~~ killed at any given moment. ~~We have~~
This is ~~what I've learned to live with,~~ what we've learned to live with.
I am aware that my children are now aware of this too. ~~We are~~ They're aware.
I am aware of how much awareness ~~I~~ we must have in order to simply exist in this country.

And then—

> Lockout at Franklin, Guerrero, and Polk lifted. All activities at the schools are now normal. EPISD police remain on campus as precaution.
>
> Txt STOP to cancel

Breathe.

This is where the chapter was supposed to end. On a single breath left alone on white space. But the day that I typed the word "breathe" was May 26, 2022. And on that day, almost at the exact moment I was writing that word, nineteen brown school children and two brown teachers were being slaughtered by a brown man in the small town of Uvalde, Texas, just south of here. Meanwhile, nineteen mostly brown cops stood outside the brown door and did nothing for more than a brown hour, except listen to the screams of the brown children and the gunfire. Strike that, they did act. But only upon the brown parents of the brown children who were desperately pleading for them to *Do something!* Tasing them. Cuffing them. Holding them at gunpoint. This is true. The brown cops. The brown parents. The brown children. The brown shooter. Have we bought into our own dehumanization? Have we become invisible to ourselves? La Matanza is alive and well in Texas. We are living in the New Hour of Blood.

V

BURY THIS HEARTACHE IN A METAPHOR

They carried all they could bear, and then some, including a silent awe for the terrible power of the things they carried.

—TIM O'BRIEN, *THE THINGS THEY CARRIED*

31

OBJECTS, EPHEMERA, AND SPACE

IN MARCH 2013, I drove Jaime Ramírez and his wife Lilia to Los Gatos Canyon, to the site of the plane crash. They were the first family that I would take. Prior to that, I had only gone alone. In those early days, I was completely directionless. I would sit on the embankment, out of sight, for hours and do nothing. Cars would pass. An occasional airplane would fly overhead. And if I was really quiet I could hear voices, so dim they seemed to come from miles away, or at times from nowhere at all. I couldn't make out what was being said, only that there was a whispering through the trees.

I led Jaime and Lilia through the barbed-wire fence, and we walked through the tall grass for about fifty yards until we reached the line of oak trees at the edge of the creek bed. I hadn't yet showed them where exactly the plane hit, but when I looked back, I found Jaime kneeling on the ground, eyes shut. He was praying. The hat he wore for this occasion had once belonged to his father, and he had placed it on the ground next to him. A minute later, he stood up, dusted off his knees, and placed the hat back on his head.

"You feel that?" I asked.

"Oh yes," he replied, "I feel it very strong."

Unknowingly, Jaime had knelt down in the very spot where the bodies had been pulled out of the creek bed. It was the location where his grandfather and uncle took their last breath.

"You're standing in the exact spot the plane crashed," I told him. Tears welled up in his eyes. Lilia comforted him. We remained silent. Words have little use in these moments.

It's difficult to grasp. How do we account for the invisible? Things we cannot see but we know exist? Radio waves. Kinetic energy. Aura. Gravity. These are a few thin phrases we've come up with. But anyone who spends time with words knows that they're merely signposts to guide us along. Words can hardly do the heavy lifting. Some things just don't make sense in the realm of language. Some things only exist in the realm of being. Gut feeling is real and physical, something each one of us is born with. This is why we can walk into a room and instantly feel the tension, or the lightness, depending on what last occurred there. This is why our bodies respond differently when placed between two mountains than between two skyscrapers. But it's more than the immediate environment. It's also the layers of what has taken place in these spaces that affect its energy. In other words, space holds memory. And so do objects.

At the R. C. Baker Museum in the small town of Coalinga, California, you can find a shorn-off piece of the propeller recovered from the plane crash site. It's the actual propeller from the very DC-3 airplane that was carrying these thirty-two souls, which smashed down in Los Gatos Canyon. But you have to ask the director Nancy Birdwell to show it to you, because it's usually kept in a back room. And when they do haul it out and place it down in front of you, you cannot deny the gravity of the object itself. Regardless of your age, gender, ethnicity, spiritual background, or political ideas, the moment they set that broken hunk of metal down in front of you, you're transported. Where to? Depends on how clear your channel is. The same goes for the Woodstock typewriter that belonged to F. J. McCollum, the first reporter on the scene. To touch the keys is to open oneself up to the trembling hands of Mr. Mac himself, frantically hammering out the headline: . . . *the worst plane crash in California's history.* You can hear his heartbeat pounding to the rhythm of the clacking keys. And always, like with every object, you cannot help but feel pulled to touch it. Go on. This is the gravity of the object itself. History is not as passive as we think it is. It calls us.

Back in 2009, when I first went to the archives of Jack Kerouac and I held the actual letters that Bea Franco had written to him sixty-two years prior, I was immediately yanked into the mystery of who she was and where she might've been. From the moment her letters grasped my fingertips she stopped being a character in a book and was now a real woman with a real history, real concerns, and hopes. Instantly humanized by the evidence of her existence. This is the power of the object. And the power of the archive. Which is why by the time Jaime Ramírez brandished the original handwritten letter that his grandfather Ramón wrote home to his wife Elisa just months before he was killed in the plane crash, I had to pause before touching it. Because I knew the instant I held Ramón's letter in my hands, there would be a shift.

Surrender.

That's the only way I can describe the feeling I got from holding Ramón's letter. As if he was already letting go. A heart anchored by regret. And I had not yet even read it. This was strictly the energy that came through by touch alone. It made sense that Ramón's spirit would be the first in line to tell me his story. In that same meeting Jaime handed me the original copy of the Spanish-language independent newspaper *El Faro.* Before touching it, I asked, "How did you get this?"

"Our family has kept it since that day."

"You've been saving it all these years?"

"That's right."

"Why?"

"For you, mi hermano. We were saving it for you."

ര

In some circles they've given it a name, "psychometry." It comes from two Greek words, *psukhē* and *metron*—*spirit measure.* Mediums also refer to it as "token-object reading." For the science geek, it's not unlike the way forensic experts can cull DNA from an object or swab an ancient footprint and tell us its story. Except in our case the tools are ancestral. And for those of faith, there is Acts 19:12: "God did extraordinary miracles through Paul, so that even handkerchiefs and aprons that had touched him were taken to the sick, and their illnesses were cured and the evil spirits left them . . ." If we wear a watch long enough, or a wedding ring, or a wallet, or our favorite boots, we leave an imprint of our energy in it. We scribble a letter to someone under strenuous circumstances, and the anxiety is there, palpable to the one who receives it. Someone snaps a photo of a person or occasion, and seventy years down the road a person touches the actual print and is suddenly overcome by a wave of emotion. Even if the object is something as simple as *blue baby clothes.*

~

The seventeenth-century Japanese poet Matsuo Bashō famously wrote: *Go to the pine if you want to learn about the pine, or to the bamboo if you want to learn about the bamboo. And in doing so, you must leave your subjective preoccupation with yourself. Otherwise you impose yourself on the object and you do not learn.*

It was during my undergraduate studies at Naropa University, a Buddhist college, that I first read this quote. This has since become my modus operandi. I've intentionally tried to seek out the people, the spaces, and the things they carried, to touch them directly with my own hand, to stand in these spaces, and record with all my senses what they have to teach me. I'm not satisfied with simply being a witness. Always, the goal is to be an active participant, if and when I can. To be the living history of this story, not merely a passive chronicler of it. The spaces I've stood in, the people I've embraced and broken bread with, and the objects I've touched and held have all come to inform my understanding. These very words are a transmission.

Partial Catalogue of Objects I Have Touched

Original copy of *El Faro* Spanish-language independent newspaper, issued March 1, 1948.

Handwritten letters (2) by Alberto Raigoza Carlos to his sister Carlota.

Handwritten letter by Ramón Paredes González to his wife Elisa.

Penny McGuire's original photographs (8) of the funeral services in 1948.

The original homes where three of the passengers once lived.

Bea Franco's handwritten letters to Jack Kerouac (5).

Virgil's wallet, ChapStick, notepad with handwritten notes.

Cassette-tape recording of Virgil's encounter with the Bakersfield PD.

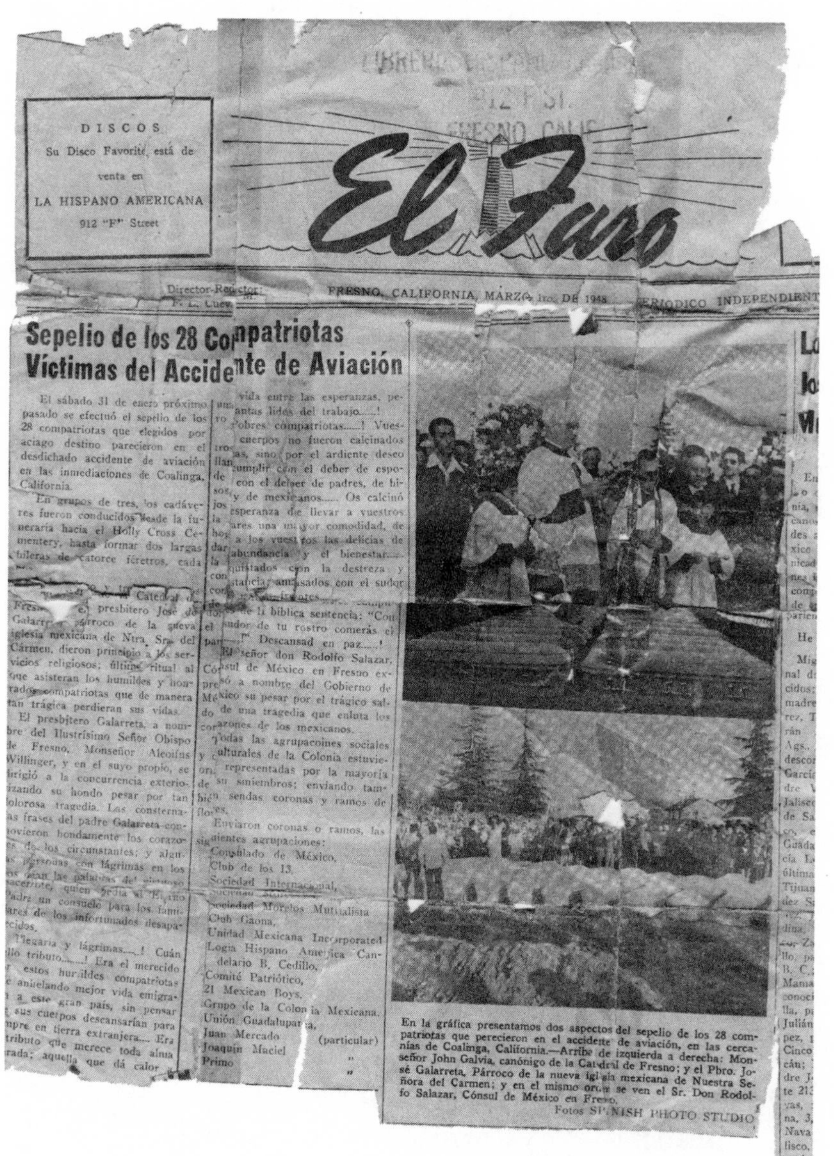

DISCOS
Su Disco Favorito está de venta en
LA HISPANO AMERICANA
912 "F" Street

El Faro

Director-Redactor: F. L. Cuev...

FRESNO, CALIFORNIA, MARZO 1ro. DE 1948

...RIODICO INDEPENDIENT...

Sepelio de los 28 Compatriotas Víctimas del Accidente de Aviación

El sábado 31 de enero próximo pasado se efectuó el sepelio de los 28 compatriotas que elegidos por aciago destino parecieron en el desdichado accidente de aviación en las inmediaciones de Coalinga, California.

En grupos de tres, los cadáveres fueron conducidos desde la funeraria hacia el Holly Cross Cementery, hasta formar dos largas hileras de catorce féretros, cada ...

... Catedral de Fresno, el presbitero José de Galarreta, párroco de la nueva iglesia mexicana de Ntra. Sra. del Cármen, dieron principio a los servicios religiosos; último ritual al que asisteran los humildes y honrados compatriotas que de manera tan trágica perdieran sus vidas.

El presbitero Galarreta, a nombre del Ilustrísimo Señor Obispo de Fresno, Monseñor Aleoíius Willinger, y en el suyo propio, se dirigió a la concurrencia exteriorizando su hondo pesar por tan dolorosa tragedia. Las consternadas frases del padre Galarreta conmovieron hondamente los corazones de los circunstantes; y algunas personas con lágrimas en los ... las palabras del ... sacerdote, quien pedia al Eterno Padre un consuelo para los familiares de los infortunados desaparecidos.

Plegaria y lágrimas.....! Cuán ... tributo......! Era el merecido ... estos humildes compatriotas ... anhelando mejor vida emigra... a este gran país, sin pensar ... sus cuerpos descansarían para ... en tierra extranjera.... Era ... tributo que merece toda alma ... rada; aquella que dá calor ...

... vida entre las esperanzas, pe... antas lides del trabajo......! Pobres compatriotas......! Vuestros cuerpos no fueron calcinados ... as, sino por el ardiente deseo ... cumplir con el deber de esposos, con el deber de padres, de hijos y de mexicanos...... Os calcinó ... esperanza de llevar a vuestros ... ares una mayor comodidad, de ... a los vuestros las delicias de ... abundancia y el bienestar... ... quistados con la destreza y ... stancia; amasados con el sudor ... frentes... ... de la biblica sentencia: "Con el sudor de tu rostro comerás el pan...!" Descansad en paz.....!

El señor don Rodolfo Salazar, Cónsul de México en Fresno expresó a nombre del Gobierno de México su pesar por el trágico saldo de una tragedia que enluta los corazones de los mexicanos.

Todas las agrupacoines sociales y culturales de la Colonia estuvieron representadas por la mayoría de su smiembros; enviando también sendas coronas y ramos de flores.

Enviaron coronas o ramos, las siguientes agrupaciones:
Consulado de México,
Club de los 13,
Sociedad Internacional,
...
Sociedad Morelos Mutualista
Club Gaona,
Unidad Mexicana Incorporated
Logia Hispano America Candelario B. Cedillo,
Comité Patriótico,
21 Mexican Boys,
Grupo de la Colonia Mexicana,
Unión Guadalupana,
Juan Mercado (particular)
Joaquin Maciel "
Primo "

En la gráfica presentamos dos aspectos del sepelio de los 28 compatriotas que perecieron en el accidente de aviación, en las cercanías de Coalinga, California.—Arribe de izquierda a derecha: Monseñor John Galvia, canónigo de la Catedral de Fresno; y el Pbro. José Galarreta, Párroco de la nueva iglesia mexicana de Nuestra Señora del Carmen; y en el mismo orden se ven el Sr. Don Rodolfo Salazar, Cónsul de México en Fresno.

Fotos SPANISH PHOTO STUDIO

Section of *El Faro* given to me by Jaime Ramírez, dated March 1, 1948.

32

A BEGINNING

My father's own father, he waded that river . . .

—WOODY GUTHRIE, "DEPORTEE (PLANE WRECK AT LOS GATOS)"

Postcard of the lynching of Laura and L. D. Nelson, circa 1911.

I AM STANDING on the banks of the North Canadian River, just outside of Okemah, Oklahoma. Woody Guthrie's hometown. We parked on the shoulder of Highway 56 to get here, then scaled a low fence and walked through a dense thicket to the banks of this river I'm now staring at. We make our way to the new bridge, a mass of concrete that stretches across the river, in this quiet, unassuming part of the world. Beneath it, the pylons are tagged with graffiti, not unlike in every city. Symbols that I can't make out at first glance, not until we get closer. Then I see they are swastikas, and a message painted in red: *Fuck N*******.

It's clear to me, history does not die. It never dies. Not here. Not anywhere. History is only reincarnated. It's always only temporarily dormant, but with the right conditions, perhaps years or decades later, it returns as something else. History is always the descendant of history. It's coded in the DNA of cities, small towns, trees, and even bridges. This is made clear to me under the Highway 56 bridge in the heart of Okfuskee County.

It's here, on this very bridge I am standing under, that on May 25, 1911, Laura Nelson and her fourteen-year-old son L. D. were lynched by a mob of white men. Young L. D. was accused of purposefully killing the local deputy sheriff. Some who witnessed the incident claim it was an accident. Others argue it was no accident at all. Regardless of the facts, what is known is that in the short days after, Laura and her son were dragged to this very bridge and hanged by the mob. I'm aware that the DNA of that incident still lives here. And I am bogged down with an indescribable grief. I was brought here by friends, the scholar Will Kaufman, the musician Joel Rafael, and his wife Lauren. There's a small group of us, but I have to walk away, give myself space for a moment.

I high-step through the tall grass, drudge carefully through the mud, careful not to slip into the river. I clutch a cattail for balance as I step to the pylons, wanting to get closer still to the graffiti. Never content with just being a viewer of things, I prefer direct interaction with the past. The closer I can get to the pylons, to the swastika and the hate, the closer I am to standing in the footprints of the human that sprayed it. And if I can stand in the footprints of the hater, perhaps I can better understand what brings a person to such hatred for what and whom they don't know. Which is also to say, the closer I will be to understanding what lies beneath my own human nature. If my search has any purpose at all, this is it. I'm trying to quell my own fires. But they're not mine alone. They are fires stoked by the embers of generations; suffering, trauma, resilience, it's all alive within me. I'm aware that every time I search for someone or something, I'm searching for pieces of myself. I am diligent about this work.

Up close, the paint is bright red, almost fresh. When I reach the closest point, I hear a sound that was surely there all along, though it took me arriving at this place to be able to hear it. Crickets. A chorus of them calling out across the river. It comes from all sides. Billions of them on these banks. And then, suddenly, the birds. Alerting one another that danger is near. I am their danger. And then the hush of trees in the light breeze. The trees look old, at least a hundred years. It's possible they stood here, as young saplings, witnessing the bodies of Laura and L. D. swinging from the bridge. And they are still whispering about it. Though this is the new bridge, there are still pieces of the original bridge left jutting out of the water, and on the banks. The crickets I am hearing in this moment are the descendants of the same crickets that sang out to Laura and L. D. on that terrible day. The birds, too, who have been in these parts for generations, could very well be descendants of the same birds that circled over the commotion of the angry mob, as they placed the nooses over the heads of Laura and L. D. And the river, of course, the river too. Even though it runs and replenishes itself, there is still something in the circular nature of its own existence that carries the genes of its ancestral incarnation. History is always the descendant of history. And I have no doubt that all of these very alive organisms, these witnesses, have something to tell me, if I listen. So I listen. The water rises up within me.

I find myself holding back tears. What is this business of holding back tears? I interrogate myself. That too is a conditioning. But I'm here to do the work, to stand in the footprints and stare the past directly in the eye. So I allow myself to feel, to really feel, unapologetically. Face it. These things have always hurt me. They have always felt deeply personal to me. I cry. I am sensitive. I've known this since day one. The men in my life have tried to cure me of this. But they didn't know it was my power. I didn't know.

But now I do. They told me, "What doesn't kill you makes you stronger." But time has taught me otherwise. What hasn't killed me has only made me softer. More malleable. Fluid. Like this river. It follows the gravity, and nothing else. Replenishing what it touches. Even my own father struggled with my sensitivity early on. Our wills were tested often. He could see that I was made soft. He's since come around in his old age, but not without our challenges. Isn't this the plight of men and their children? Fatherhood. How to forget the pain of our past, and extract the light of now? Sometimes we can't. Sometimes we must dissent from our own conditioning. From that which our own parents believed was love, but was in truth love's silent cousin, fear.

It's no secret that Woody Guthrie's father, Charles Guthrie, was a part of the mob that lynched Laura Nelson and her son L. D. Nor that he was a card-carrying member of the Ku Klux Klan and a white supremacist. Before mother and son were dragged to the North Canadian River bridge, they had spent some days in the local Okemah jailhouse. This before the mob assembled. The lore is that passersby could hear Laura crying out, "Please don't kill my baby and my son!" Woody was born a year later. He would grow up seeing this lynching on postcards in his small town, peddled as souvenirs. The inhumane treatment of people who were of a different race or color left an imprint on his spirit. He went on his own search. Traversed the country as a hobo, singing at Okie and Mexican labor camps, immersing himself wholly in the lives of the Other. He would find reconciliation in music. Later in life, once he knew exactly on which side of his father's beliefs he stood, he committed himself to writing songs that opposed everything that Charles Guthrie had once advocated. Songs that gave names to the nameless and stories to the storyless. "Deportee (Plane Wreck at Los Gatos)" is just one of hundreds. Standing in his father's footprints, he had become intimate with hate. Standing in the footprints of the Other, he had become intimate with love. And if that wasn't enough to soften him and add fuel to his convictions, the hard lessons he'd gather from fatherhood were.

February 9, 1947

It is one year *before* the plane crash at Los Gatos Canyon. On this afternoon, Woody attends a rally for the United Electrical Workers at the Phelps Dodge plant in New Jersey. He doesn't plan to stay long. It's his daughter Cathy Ann's fourth birthday. She's the gem of his eye, and his muse. The two are practically inseparable. He calls her "Little Miss Stackabones." He's written numerous children's songs for her, even includes her in some of his recordings. All he wants is to get back home to celebrate Little Miss Stackabones with cake and a proper party.

When he returns home that evening, instead of finding a house bursting with children's laughter, he discovers it empty. There's been a fire. His wife Marjorie summons him to the hospital, and he rushes over. It's little Cathy Ann. She's been in an accident. Her dress caught fire from a spark that came from their radio. She's burned profusely. Just days after she had turned four, little Cathy Ann is dead.

Woody is inconsolable. He slips into a darkness. Doesn't speak or eat. His friends will try getting him out of the house for some air. They take him for a walk on the beach. He throws himself onto the sand and kicks and howls endlessly. And then the anger sets in. One year *before* the plane crash at Los Gatos, Woody gathers himself up and does what he's always done in these unbearable moments: he turns to words. But in this instant, little does he know just how prophetic what he's about to put down on paper will become. On March 6, 1947, he writes a letter to his friend John Lomax, in which he vents over what happened to his little Cathy Ann:

> *. . . the spark was caused by a faulty no good wartime radio wire, which shows that the cheap synthetic imitation products made for the greedy profits of a manufacturer is still failing us in a million ways, in ship hulls, in brake shoes . . .* ***and in the airplanes that fall down from their upper places to fill our papers and our radio speakers with only some dim echo of the living eyes and faces that get marked out in their fall.***

Ten months after writing these words Woody's prophecy comes true. A Douglas DC-3 airplane deporting twenty-eight Mexicans "falls down from its upper place and fills our radio speakers with only a dim echo of the living eyes and faces that get marked out . . ." After which they are buried in a mass unmarked grave, where they'll remain anonymous for more than seventy years.

It's clear to me now. By the time the plane crash occurred, Woody had already begun writing this song. The words were in his DNA. In its own way, the death of his most beloved, Little Miss Stackabones, was the springboard, and the rage, and the fuel behind what would come later. He was now intimate with the dark spiral of loss, and with the system responsible for it. And he had begun searching for the words. The plane crash at Los Gatos was just the invitation.

When you experience loss at this magnitude, the new direction your heart takes will apply to everything. To all losses and heartbreaks thereafter. And wherever that fire occurs, it becomes your mission to extinguish it. Everything becomes a metaphor for addressing the original wound. When you listen to "Plane Wreck at Los Gatos" through this filter, you realize its subject is much greater than a plane crash. Encoded within the lyrics is a man seeking dignity for all people, inviting us to question how we make decisions and to consider whom our decisions affect. And he himself is not exempt from this narrative. In the original handwritten lyrics, Woody writes:

Is this my best way I can grow my big orchard?
Is this my best way I can grow my good fruit?

Throughout the song he uses the first-person *I*, and only later it is changed to the collective *we*. He's aware that his personal history cannot be ignored in relation to the plane crash. He intuits the interconnectedness of both. The death of his beloved Cathy Ann is tied to the plane crash, and to his racist father, and to himself. The same human plague has touched all their lives in one form or another. Invisibility. As a father, I can no longer listen to "Deportee (Plane Wreck at Los Gatos)" and not hear it as a love letter to his child. To all of our children. Just because the lyrics of the song are not addressed to them doesn't mean it isn't true. A father will do that. Bury his own heartache in a metaphor so that his children do not see the original wound.

ᘓ

In 2014, I attended the Woody Guthrie Music Festival that is held annually in Okemah. I was given access to the backstage area and was making my way toward the buffet tent, where they had lunch waiting for us. I was already imagining myself knee-deep in hummus when I suddenly found myself standing face-to-face with Arlo Guthrie, the folk icon and musical heir to his father's throne. And though Joan Baez sang my favorite version of "Deportee (Plane Wreck at Los Gatos)," it was Arlo's version that I had grown up hearing. My dad was a fan and often sang Arlo's songs out loud around the house.

I introduced myself to Arlo, and he replied, in his familiar, jovial voice, "You're the guy who found the deportees, aren't ya?"

I was surprised he'd heard about my work, since my book had not yet come out. "That's me," I said, trying not to sound like a complete goof.

"That's a wonderful thing you did, that's just . . ." he folded his arms across his chest, which indicated he was genuinely having a conversation with me, "that's incredible. Now how many of those families have ya found so far?"

I knew that number by heart, yet in this moment it eluded me. I counted in my head.

"Three," I said.

"Is that right?" He paused a moment and stared directly into my eyes. "I'm just curious . . . what made ya want to go looking for those people? What got ya started with all that?"

VI

THIS PLAGUE OF INVISIBILITY

We tell ourselves stories in order to live,
or to justify taking a life, even our own . . .
—REBECCA SOLNIT, *THE FARAWAY NEARBY*

33

THE CASSETTE TAPE (#1)

2017

MY MOM hands me a cassette tape. It's clear, with the label "Memorex DBS" on one side and the colors yellow and pink on the other.

"What's this?"

"I think it's your uncle."

I know she means Virgil.

"What's in it?"

She tilts her head. "I think it's the recording of when the police dogs attacked him."

She's referring to an incident with the Kern County Sheriff's Department that happened twenty-three years earlier.

"How'd you get this?"

"I've had it."

"No, I mean how'd you get a recording of that incident?"

My mom lowers the volume on the television.

"Virgil called me earlier that morning. He knew something was up. He said he wanted our phone number to be the last one he called, so that if anything happened he could just hit speed dial. So later that afternoon the phone rang and I picked it up and I could hear him. His voice and the cops. It was awful. My first reaction was to hit the record button on the answering machine, and I ended up getting the whole thing on tape. I forgot about it all these years, but just the other day I was looking for something and came across it. I thought maybe you'd want it. I don't remember what that tape looked like, but something tells me that's it."

"You didn't hear it?"

"No. And I don't want to."

34

VIRGIL

Bang, bang, bang, bang, bang
then blame, blame, blame
it's not my thing, so let it go . . .

THESE LYRICS are by the alternative rock band R.E.M. The song, "Bang and Blame," was released in the fall of 1994 and appears as track 8 on their album *Monster.* I was working for the Wherehouse music store, back when music had to be purchased from such places. A perk of the job was selling concert tickets—my real motivation for working there. I was twenty-one.

On May 17, 1995, Alejandra and I drove to the Shoreline Amphitheatre in Mountain View, California, to see R.E.M. in concert. It was a Wednesday, and the trip was going to be a quick turnaround. My mom's birthday was in two days, May 19, so I wanted to be back the very next day. Alejandra and I went and had a great time. We stayed for R.E.M.'s entire set but left just before the encore. It was a long show, and I recall "Bang and Blame" coming in at around the halfway mark, because it was the only song I really liked on that album. Beneath the stars we sang:

If you could see yourself now, baby
It's not my fault, you used to be so in control
You're going to roll right over this one
Just roll me over and let me go, you're laying blame . . .

Singing this song under the open sky with Alejandra would be my last clear memory of spring 1995. After this night the sequence of events in my life over the next days and months become a blur. Here is what I'm able to recall. I recall the amphitheater not being too far from the ocean. I recall the cool air against our sweaty faces, and the both of us feeling ethereal, like somehow age would never catch us. After the concert we got a hotel room, stayed the night, and started back to Visalia around noon the next day. It's a four-hour drive from the bay to Visalia without traffic, so I must've walked through the front door around 4:00 or 5:00 p.m. When I arrived Virgil had just gotten home from work and was still in the shower. His friend Sam was sitting in his truck outside, waiting. They were going out. Mom stuck her head out the door and told Sam he could come inside and wait for Virgil, but Sam declined. A minute later Virgil exited the bathroom in a cloud of steam, shirtless, slicking his hair back with his hand. I could tell he was in a hurry because he looked at me and said, "You're back, huh," as he headed to his room without waiting for my response.

I was sitting in the kitchen, watching Mom make her legendary potato salad. Dad was out back putting steaks on the grill. Virgil came down the hallway dressed in jeans and a white tank top; the scent of Zest body soap hung in the air. Who knew it would be the last scent I had of my uncle?

"When do you get baby Eric again, tío?"

"Shit, I don't know, mijo. I'm trying to work that out with his mom."

"Virgil, you don't wanna stay and eat before you go?" Mom asked.

"Nah, carnala, Sam and I are gonna grab something."

"He can come inside and eat too." Mom was relentless. Especially when it came to her baby brother. Virgil must've cracked a joke because I remember her laughing. I remember all of us laughing. We laughed a lot with Virgil.

The door closed behind him and he was gone. Just like that.

I want to say that I heard Virgil's truck door slam, and that I listened to him drive away. Or that I remembered the joke he cracked that had us all laughing, but that's not the truth. In order to remember, I would've had to have been paying attention. But the moment he shut the front door I had already moved on. I probably began stuffing my face. I probably sang, *Bang bang, then blame blame,* then threw myself onto the couch and clicked on the television. Whatever it was, I'm sure it was the exact opposite of paying attention. I think of this often: if I had known that was the last time I was going to see my uncle, I would've paid more attention.

12:30 a.m., or Thereabouts

For many years I've attempted to describe in writing the sound of my mother's wail. But words don't do it justice. It yanked me out of a deep sleep. At first I thought it was a dream, but it came again. From down the hall. Closer to the living room. I leapt to the door, and from the hall I could see Mom slumped on the ground, shaking uncontrollably. Dad held on to her. I ran to them, and that's when they appeared. The Visalia Police Department. Several officers gathered at our front door. The door I had last seen Virgil shut. A chaplain dressed in black looked coldly at me. Mom shouted, "My baby brother! Virgil!"

"What?" I said. "What happened?" I looked at my dad, his eyes were vacant.

The chaplain put his hand on my shoulder. His badge was clipped to his belt.

"I'm sorry," he said, his voice like a still pond. "Virgil Zuñiga passed."

"You killed him!" Mom moaned. "My baby brother. You fuckin' killed him!"

"What?" I looked at the chaplain. "What happened?"

"I'm sorry," he said. The other officers stepped outside.

"Where is he?"

The chaplain ignored my question. Mom sobbed. I got on my knees and held her and Dad. A minute later my sister Dee came out rubbing her eyes. We all held each other, and the world around us became nonexistent. At some point the chaplain left too, and then it was just us. My mother would not stop trembling.

"Honey," Dad said, "honey!" He held on to her with both arms.

But Mom was gone. She had turned inward. Her silence was deafening. The woman Dad thought he was holding wasn't there. I could see it in her eyes and in the shape her body took. Mom was childlike. Dad was holding Chita in his arms. We all were. Mom began to speak Virgil's name. Over and over, invoking him to reappear. We sat there, on the floor of our living room, cradling Chita, hanging on tight to one another. All of us, calling his name out loud. Expecting his return. But he never did. Not in that moment. At some point the sun rose. And when it did, Chita had turned forty-two. It was Mom's birthday. We didn't celebrate. The candles were already blown out.

Years later, I managed to procure footage of that night captured by a local news channel minutes after it happened. The images are grainy and certain shots are without audio. There are only four scenes, stitched together with jump cuts:

The first clip is soundless. The time code shows 11:17 p.m. Virgil is dead. His body on a gurney, being stuffed into the back of an ambulance. Lights flash.

The next clip is also silent. Two Visalia PD officers are discussing the situation with a man in plain clothes directly in front of the house, and we see the scene is quarantined with yellow caution tape.

The third clip has sound, and it's the morning after the incident. An eyewitness with a mullet and sunglasses is telling the camera what he heard: He was saying he didn't care what happened, he wasn't gonna give up . . . shoot me if you want . . . I don't care . . .

Now we see the front window of the house Virgil once lived in with his wife. But for the last several months, only she lived there, with the children. There is a close-up on the window screen. A bullet hole.

Black out.

Here is exactly how it all went down. Here is the story.

A few months before, baby Eric's mother took legal action to get full custody of the boy, and Virgil, understandably, went ballistic. He wasn't about to lose a son. Not again. A week away from their court date, he grows fearful and desperate. In a drunken attempt to retrieve his son, he leaps the back fence of her house, bangs on the door, and demands that she give baby Eric to him. Neighbors threaten to call the cops, but he's not going anywhere, not without his son. Not this time. He busts the door open. She scrambles out the front. The Visalia PD arrives. And now Virgil is barricaded in the house with the little boy. The cops shout at him to surrender, but he tells them to go fuck themselves. He's not leaving without his son. If the choices are either lose a son or die, he prefers death. The window curtains are slightly parted, and when the sharpshooter sees his brown body walk past he takes aim and fires. All within fifteen minutes, from the second they arrive to the time my uncle is killed. The cops claim he had a knife, but when they approach his body there is no knife. He was unarmed and appeared to be reaching for the telephone. In fact, the telephone receiver is found lying next to him on the floor. My mother believes he was going to call her. And because I have received many such late-night calls from Virgil, I believe this too.

This is the version I have told myself *in order to live.*

ത

But there are multiple truths.

Another is that the baby's mother had taken out a restraining order against Virgil because he had been violent with her in front of the children, and she needed to protect herself and them.

Still another's truth, perhaps that of an eyewitness with no loyalty to anyone involved, could be that Virgil called it upon himself by taunting the Visalia PD.

And still again, perhaps there are a few who know too well the degree of darkness my uncle was truly capable of, who might suggest it was karma. Virgil had it coming.

And if we take a step farther back, through a more compassionate lens, we could say Virgil had never overcome the wounds he experienced as a child. The ghosts of New Mexico loom.

Whatever the viewpoint, or "truth," each of these is valid to the one who needs it.

ത

And yet, none of this reconciles how much the untimely death of my uncle would change the trajectory of my life. Nor can it erase the love I held for him. The only factual thing I know is that in his thirty-eighth year, the uncle I had loved like a brother for most of my life was killed.

Since May 18, 1995, I have spent all of my waking hours paying attention.

On that day, a monstrous silence consumed me. It was so overbearing that I developed a subtle ringing in my ears that sometimes returns to this day. This is what the mind does. When something is missing, it seeks out. In my case, I deliberately sought words. They could not do the heavy lifting, but they offered me a way to reflect. To see what I was not seeing. I began scribbling words onto my paintings. Later, into a sketchbook. And then, when I dared, into a journal. One day a complete stranger pointed at these written thoughts and called it "poetry." It had a name. I would do more of this, much more. Through writing I could survive the grief. Through writing I would learn how to pay attention.

This was the beginning.

11:17PM
CAUTION
CAUTION

35

THE FLY

IN A LETTER dated July 2, 1964, my grandmother Magdalena writes to her sister Apolonia:

> *Polly, I hate to have to write all my troubles out to you, but I have nobody else to write to . . . I don't know why we have been so unlucky.*

In her despair, my grandmother too turned to words. She admits to writing out her troubles and to seeking a reader. An alignment that is not lost on me. What she couldn't know in this moment is that one year after composing this letter, she would succumb to breast cancer.

Perhaps my grandfather Alejandro was right to shoo the butterfly out of the house that day. Perhaps his belief in omens was not farfetched after all. Because six months before Virgil was killed it had returned.

The fly.

The same one that landed on the wound slashed across my grandmother's left breast in 1964, the one that little Chita was responsible for keeping away, had returned once again. This time it had come to claim Chita. A curse thirty years in the making. In November of 1994 my mother was informed by her doctor that her tests revealed she had breast cancer.

She would begin treatments of chemotherapy immediately. A procedure that kept her nauseous and vomiting daily. In the following weeks she grew frail and lost an incredible amount of weight. The long, thick Sophia Loren hair my mom was always known for had fallen out. But more than its physical toll, coping with the same curse that took her own mother yanked her back to that part of her past, and all the fears that came with it. Having lost her mom at a young age, raised herself and her siblings, witnessed her father drown in a bottle, lost control of everything and everyone, little Chita now found herself inside a grown woman's body, staring down God and her own mortality. But this time was different. This time Chita would take matters into her own hands. She refused to let the fly win this time. She wouldn't allow herself to be a victim. Fear of death becomes need for control but manifests as anxiety masquerading as anger. Her determination was scary. I remember it clearly. My mother was unstoppable. For months we watched her force herself out of bed most days, get dressed, and go about with some hell-bent level of normalcy. And it was working. Until that night when the police came knocking on our door.

This is the state my mother was in when her baby brother Virgil was killed. This is the state she was in when she howled that night. This is what she was howling at. On the outside, physically fighting for her own life. On the inside, quarreling with God about an inheritance she never asked for.

36

THE MEDICINE OF OPEN ROADS

2020

IN MY REARVIEW MIRROR I see the mountains that divide Mexico from the United States fade across the skyline and disappear. Out in front of me there is nothing but a flat line. This is the direction I am heading. Flatline, Texas. Eastbound.

I pull onto the shoulder of Interstate 10 and climb out of my truck to stretch. I stand for a moment and take in the hot desert air. I stare at a gargantuan chaparral looming nearby, say my hellos, and she nods. Gobernadora. The Governess. She goes by many names. We are both natural observers. We pay attention. Of course, I'm new to this. She isn't. She has known this for centuries. She knows how to make the most of whatever the situation presents. She does not shy away or seek to escape. She welcomes the storm by spreading her arms and absorbing whatever comes her way. She stores the rain for bleak days ahead when water is scarce. And when that day comes she folds her branches and turns inward, preserving her energy. I am learning.

This day is a scorcher. I take my water bottle and splash my face and hair. Diesels fly past, and I think of my father. This is his route, central California into the gut of Texas. At the age of eleven, his dad pulled him from a baseball game in the Rio Grande valley, threw him in the back of a pickup truck, and off they went, leaving Texas in the rearview for good.

From that moment on he would come to call this route home. When I say this is my father's route, I mean this stretch of highway is one of his inheritances. And so it is one of mine. Except that my father has long since known what has taken me most of my adult life to learn. That driving long distances is where we find our peace. In the space between point A and point Z there exists a parenthesis. A pause. Life on hold. The road is sanity. It is without expectation. It only demands one thing of you. To pay attention. To be present. A highway is a stream of present moment upon present moment. The tires lap against the road chanting now, now, now, now. And yet, when the road is good and the stretch long, I am also pulled back by then, then, then.

෴

When I think of my mother's resilience, I think of my father's too.

Just months after Virgil was killed, Dad lost his job in the auto finance industry. They were downsizing, and because he only had a ninth-grade education, he was the first to be let go. Our upward mobility was short-lived. My mother was still at war with cancer, now Virgil was dead, and for the first time in their entire lives my parents were unable to secure work. They refused to start over again. Which for them meant back to the fields. In a desperate move, they took what meager savings they had and attempted to open a used-car lot in the town of Tulare. For good luck, my father named the lot after the home he had been yanked from so long ago, *Rio Grande Motors.* I would see very little of this business because I ran as far away from Visalia as I could. Not long after it opened its doors, Rio Grande Motors was robbed, and soon after this they closed the doors permanently. We had lost it all. No money. No prospects. A heavy depression set in. Sporadically, I would visit my parents and sleep in my old bedroom, then leave bright and early the next day. The echoes of Virgil's death haunted the hallways, and I felt suffocated if I stayed longer than twenty-four hours.

Early one morning, when it was still dark out, I had heard a noise coming from my parents' kitchen. I crept out of bed and slowly walked down the hall to see what it was. I could hear the stirring of life, but I couldn't see anyone or anything. A small dim light was on. I crept closer still. As I reached the kitchen, I saw a body hunched over in a chair. A tattered flannel shirt, and dirty jeans. It was moving slowly, quietly. I stepped closer, not knowing if it was real or if I was dreaming. As I inched forward, I could see the body was lacing up an old pair of work boots. On the floor, next to his boots, was a dirty set of field-hand gloves. He felt my presence and looked up at me.

"Mijo," he said. "What're you doing up?"

It was my dad.

"Where're you going?" I whispered. He reached for his gloves.

"To work."

"What work?"

"I got a job."

"Where?"

He hesitated. "Picking cotton out in Coalinga." He wouldn't look me in the eye.

"The fields?"

My father hadn't set foot in a field in almost fifteen years. He snatched his thermos off the counter. "Gotta make money somehow." He checked his pocket for his keys, then headed out the front door. And just like that, he was gone. I stood for several minutes inside the weight of his decision. I knew what it must've taken for him to swallow his pride and return to the fields. The place of his own beginning.

@

I continue eastward on I-10, pass the hills of Balmorhea, and then later Sonora, where I dodge a family of plump javelinas attempting to cross to the other side of the highway. How these defenseless beasts have survived in this hard terrain for more than 50 million years is beyond me. They were revered by the Maya and kept for ritual and food, a fact that I haven't researched and don't intend to. To just look at them is to see that they are ancestral to this land, and inherently worthy of our respect.

Dusk arrives. I watch the sun reach its orange arm across the dashboard the way my grandfather once did, tapping on the compass during our long migrations, field to field, season upon season. Those were the rare moments I got to sit in the cab of his truck. Usually my cousins and I were piled in the bed, making a fort of the camper shell, where we laughed and dreamed and spent many nights staring out the windows at these same highways, and at night, the endless galaxies. Of course, it was never this romantic. Not with half a dozen campesino kids slumped over one another, licking their unbrushed teeth, farting, letting their sodden socks air out, bickering, annoyed at one another, pushing, cussing out loud. Until the purr of our machine floating down the highway lulled us to sleep. We made the best of it, and so did our parents. These were the earliest migrations, recorded in every muscle of my being. *This is more the work of a poet than a trained oral historian . . . my only real credentials for having written it were that I was native to its situation in nearly every way and had only to listen to hear my own world talking.* When I consider what brought me to this story of the plane crash at Los Gatos, I hear these words by Ronald Blythe, the Englishman who documented the testimonies of his dying village in Suffolk.

Perhaps, in some way, I am still chasing after that purr. Which is to say, *that sound of my own world talking*, and that deep sense of home that I found in the back of my grandfather's truck. A campesino child, I have seen many long roads and have basked in the parenthesis for the greater part of my life.

Once, when I was still new to fatherhood, we had been visiting friends in Jemez Pueblo when we were informed that a blizzard was headed our way. If we didn't leave right away we'd be stuck there for days. We cut our visit short, piled into the car, and made a beeline up Interstate 25, northbound, in the direction of our home in Boulder, Colorado. Everyone was asleep while I drove. The first few hours my nerves were a wreck. The wind was blasting a white sheet of snow across the windshield, blinding my view. I pushed on, praying our car would hold out. But by the fourth hour, after the worst had passed, the sky split open, and suddenly a full, lavender moon appeared in the darkness. It was now past midnight, and the road was barren. The moon was so vibrant that it felt pointless to have my headlights on, so I turned them off and drove only with the soft glow to guide me. After my eyes adjusted, the panorama of snowy dunes appeared like a purple-hued blanket. The stars sparkled, punctuating the silence. No wind. Not even the wheels could be heard against the soft snowy asphalt. It was a soundless drive. We were aloft, inside the night. Inside the parenthesis. A clarity like none I had ever experienced.

At around Junction my cell service cuts out. I want to look up the distance to Corpus Christi, but I take it as a sign. I am searching for my purpose. What is it that I am driving toward? What pulls me this way? I suspected it was my grandmother Estela, pointing me back to Corpus. To her beginning. But now I'm not so sure. I keep driving, spitting cherry pits out the window, contemplating.

I was once madly in love with a woman from this part of Texas. Countless times I drove this very route. She was my last heartbreak. We were good drinking partners. Six years into clarity and now I see it for what it was, an illusion. The two are entangled. Let me rewrite that. The love was mad. More like the collision of broken hearts. She was recently divorced, and I was now a single father, stateless and in between lives. Neither of us in a place to love. We sought numbness. And we assured one another heavy doses of it. Debauchery. Sex. Dagger words. Long silences. We were the mirror of all we distrusted within ourselves. The kind of diluvio alcohol alone was incapable of. So we made a cocktail of the two and drowned our pasts with it. How romantic. At the time, I needed to be soul-numb, and what better way to forget one pain than to feel another pain. Like having someone stomp on your foot to ease your headache. Relief. But what a hell of a way to live, rolling one pain atop the other. What you end up with is a sarcophagus, buried beneath the very walls you have built with your own two hands. But this is the only type of love I was familiar with. I was conditioned to navigate brokenness in the name of love. To put up walls and permit no one to pass. The mere idea that love could be peaceful was bullshit, a myth.

But I am not there anymore. I am elsewhere.

And yet, still, without reason, the geography calls me. So I go. I drive and drive, knowing full well there's nothing and no one waiting for me in that direction anymore. But this is when the driving is best. A mysterious gravity. And an open road without expectation. This is when the living is best. I imagine this is what the Coahuiltecas before me had sought. Nomadic, perhaps they had heard of Yanaguana's healing waters and migrated east, on a route they had inherited from their fathers. Guided by their grandmothers' beginnings. Guided by a mirage of love. Not knowing that the walls of the Alamo, which they would be made to build, would one day become their grave. Perhaps, with each step, they too felt as if they were getting closer to something.

37

THE CASSETTE TAPE (#2)

2017

A FEW WEEKS have passed since Mom gave me the cassette tape. I'm finally able to sit down with it alone. That Virgil had thought to hit speed-dial in a quick instant. That my mom had thought to hit record in a quick instant. What did it say about us? That the instinctual reflex of our family was to document what might happen, what is happening, and what had already happened. And this before cell phones.

I will listen to this tape now. With no one else in the house but me. I bought a cassette player just for this moment. I slide the cassette in and press play.

It begins—

Virgil screams. He's shouting someone's name. Or names. Dogs are barking. Commotion. Grunts and banging. The door, or what I assume is a door, is kicked in. Dogs attack. I can hear them. A hard thud. Virgil drops to the floor. Screams, *Get them off me! Get them . . . gahh!* He's half crying, half screaming. The dogs tear at his flesh, his pants, his face. They're relentless. Where are the cops? I only hear Virgil screaming, and the dogs. I can feel the tremor rise up in me. That's enough. I press stop. I don't want to invite this into my body. I'll put the cassette tape away and never listen to it again. My therapist is right. If I'm to ever move on, I must stop reliving the past. I'm capable of this. I can do this, stay present. But then there are days when it feels as if the past seeks me out.

38

TREMORS

2017

I AWOKE TO the sound of a loud bang. I was sure *they* had returned. It was three in the morning. I leapt up and hurried to the front door thinking this time I'd catch them. I heard voices outside, and so I peeked through the window. A gray car rolled to a stop in the middle of the intersection in front of my house. By the light of the streetlamp, I could vaguely see the driver. He was wearing a white shirt and was slumped with his head leaning against the half-open window. Seconds later, another man emerged from a yard, ran to the car, opened the door, and attempted to shake the driver. He backed away and called out to someone. A woman appeared. She peeked into the car and covered her mouth. I cracked my window open slightly to hear what they were saying.

"Call 911!" the man shouted. She bolted off. I went to find my phone and make the call myself, but by the time I found it a police car had arrived. That fast. The driver was unconscious. Two officers pulled him from the vehicle and placed his body on the ground. Blood drenched the man's shirt. He'd been shot. In front of my house. The officers called out to him. Minutes later, an ambulance arrived. No sirens. Only the spinning lights. I couldn't watch any more. I shut the blinds and sat on my bed. Adrenaline coursed through me. I was suddenly nervous. I went to check on Salvador and Rumi, and both were sound asleep. It was real.

In late 2004, when Rumi was just a few weeks old and we were living in Fresno, a teenager named Johnny Tapia was shot and killed in our front yard. At the angle he was standing, the bullet tore through his chest and was stopped only by the steel fence post on our driveway. Had the fence post not been there it would have traveled directly into Rumi's bedroom, possibly her window. For as long as we lived in that house, the hole in the fence would be a menacing reminder.

In the days and weeks after, Johnny's family lit candles and camped on our sidewalk. Some nights they played music. Some nights they cried. They pinned balloons, flowers, and photographs on our fence. The entrance to our home had become their grief altar. They were a constant presence. Sometimes one. Sometimes several. There's something about touching the last known location of a loved one that calls to us. We're drawn to the portals of last exit. We need to stand inside of the space. I know this too well, so I never once considered asking them to leave. Despite the fact that each evening their presence took me back to the moment of Virgil's death. They were welcome to stay as long as they needed to.

Years after Johnny Tapia's death, it would happen again. And again. Killings that I would be made to witness, on television or social media. At the hands of the police. At the hands of others. At the hands of our own. My body cannot discriminate between murders. That is for the work of the mind. The body experiences them as one.

Virgil. George Floyd. Jakelin Caal. Twenty-three at Walmart. Ten in Buffalo. Nineteen children in Uvalde, Texas, abandoned by those sworn to protect them. Police shoot a man seven times in front of his children, and the news repeats: *In front of his children.* I refuse to watch the leaked footage of the children witnessing their father's murder. I refuse to witness the dehumanization process unfolding. I made that mistake once in 2020. It was a video that I was pulled to. But that was an entirely different circumstance. That one contained words. More than images, it was what the young man said that lured me to view it.

Elijah McClain.

It was different because in Elijah's final moment of desperation his language becomes incantatory. The words are tender, and in that tenderness is a deep, resonant power. The quality of his boyish innocence is still there. And it's in the boy's innocence that I hear my own son, Salvador, when he's done nothing wrong but is being accused and made to defend himself. I see my boy, nervous, stumbling to find the right words. And it pains me. In his will to survive, Elijah demonstrates compassion toward his violators, the police officers, as he's being assaulted. To read the transcript aloud is to set off the incantation—a spell from the soul being cast out urgently into the cold Colorado sky. Not only to his assailants, but to the future unnamed assailants who will undoubtedly find their way into our news feeds to come. If you pay attention closely, you can hear the boy desperately seeking the words. He begins, where else but with his name—

My name is Elijah McClain . . .
That's my house . . .
I was just going home . . .
I'm an introvert . . .
I'm just different. That's all . . .
I'm, I'm so sorry . . .
I, I have no gun . . .
I don't do that stuff . . .
I don't do any fighting . . .
Why are you attacking me?
I don't even kill flies . . .
I don't eat meat!
But I don't judge people . . .
I don't judge people who do eat meat . . .
Forgive me . . .
All I was trying to do was become better . . .
I will do it. I will do anything . . .
Sacrifice my identity . . .
I'll do it . . .
You're all phenomenal . . .
You're beautiful . . .
and I love you. Try
and forgive me . . .

Read that again. Out loud, so that your body can engage with what is happening.

Young Elijah is attempting to make himself visible.

And he attempts this, not by rendering the police officers invisible with disrespect or profanity, but by calling them in to his own circle of visibility. In his incantation he reflects back to them an elemental truth, that they are "phenomenal," and he begs them to "try." He even goes on to encourage them: *Teamwork makes the dream work!* His only goal here is to be seen as a human among humans. Even at the cost of *sacrificing his identity*. He owes the cops no grace, and yet the amount of grace he is offering them as he's being killed is almost saintly. But this will not be enough to spare him. Just as it would not have been enough to spare my uncle.

In the prologue to his book *Invisible Man*, Ralph Ellison first informed us of this plague of invisibility: *No, I am not a spook like those who haunted Edgar Allan Poe; nor am I one of your Hollywood-movie ectoplasms. I am a man of substance, of flesh and bone, fiber and liquids—and I might even be said to possess a mind. I am invisible, understand, simply because people refuse to see me.*

It's this plague of invisibility that has tainted humanity since the beginning. I do not see the murders of Virgil, Elijah McClain, George Floyd, Jakelin Caal, the Walmart victims, or nineteen school children in Uvalde as separate from the victims of the plane crash at Los Gatos. I assure you it is this same plague that made it possible for twenty-eight Mexicans to be rendered nameless in death by the very system that employed them. By the very system that benefited from their labor. How do twenty-eight brown people end up buried anonymously in a mass grave, thousands of miles from home, without their families being notified or having any knowledge of where their remains rest? How does a black man get murdered in broad daylight, in front of his children, by those sworn to protect him? No doubt the same way a seven-year-old Guatemalan child can die while in custody. And if it is okay that a single child dies while in custody, and it is okay that a few children can witness their father being killed, then it's not a stretch to imagine we will soon allow a classroom filled with nineteen children to be slaughtered while more than a dozen heavily armed men—fathers, sons, brothers—all "sworn to protect" stand just feet away and remain indifferent to the massacre. How does this happen? How is it possible?

People refuse to see me.

We are made to witness, and to succumb to, and relive within our bodies, this plague of invisibility time and again. And though the people who appear on my television screen or newsreels are unknown to me, nor do I know their personal history, every single time I'm made to witness these deaths, these blatant acts of dehumanization, I am sent a message: This could have been me. Strike that. The message is: This *is* happening to me. Tell my body otherwise. The footage, the screams, the raw anguish—I tremble at the sight of it, and the urge to come undone rises to the surface. The sudden rush of fear. The "irrational" bolt of anger. The need to escape, to lash out, break away. It consumes me, for an instant, and I am powerless over it. And when I am powerless, I'm afraid. And when I'm afraid, my reflex is to seize control, to take the power back, and nothing and no one will stand in the way of this. It's taken me most of my lifetime to understand this, and more importantly, to see it coming. The rage. It trembles from somewhere deep. The only way to quell this, I am learning, is to spot it before it takes hold. To pay close attention to the tremors long before the quake. And then to sit down with it and acknowledge where it lives in my body. Investigate where this sensation is stored in my muscles and bones. Locate the wound, the source. Touch it gently and don't turn away. No matter how much I want to, don't. To numb myself with alcohol or other vices is to allow it to take up further residence inside me. And then stare it in the eye until it is emptied of its power. And then walk myself slowly back out into the light. With each step, will myself toward an outcome different from anger, or violence, or escape. This requires a heightened form of paying attention. Which requires clarity. And then, once it passes, and it will, I return again to my truest self. It isn't easy. Admitting we hurt. Admitting we are wounded. This isn't relegated to any one gender or race. This is something we all have in common. No one is exempt from suffering. And it's an unfortunate truth that these traumas, these inheritances, which we did not ask for, are ours now to shed. Locating the medicine is our work to do. And so we must search for it.

VII

WITNESS

People are trapped in history and history is trapped in them.

—JAMES BALDWIN, "STRANGER IN THE VILLAGE"

39

CARACOL

Cry cry cry crycrycrycrycrycrycry . . .
Let your sobs cast you off, fuse into
radio, television, radar, give repeated
testimony of the Massacre . . .

—LIAO YIWU, "MASSACRE"

൭

BEIJING, CHINA, 1989. Thousands of students gather at Tiananmen Square to protest the government. The People's Liberation Army has descended upon the square, and chaos ensues. Nearby, a thirty-year-old poet named Liao Yiwu is listening to the commotion on the radio. He can feel the tension boiling. Words come to him. With the radio in the background, he composes a fire in the shape of a prayer disguised as a poem. He knows it will never be accepted for publication. He doesn't care. It's needed right now. He performs the work, then and there, recording it onto a cassette tape. He chants and howls, and rattles an abacus, and uses ritualistic cadence to invoke the spirits of the dead. He calls the piece "Massacre." In his voice you can hear his rage unfolding:

Open fire! Fire! . . .
Smash a skull open!
Fry the skin on his head to a crisp!
Make the brain gush out! . . .
Run quickly, son! . . .
Uncle. Auntie. Grandpa. Granny. Daddy. Mummy.
How much farther 'til we're home?

We have no home . . . home is a comforting desire.
Let us die in this desire . . .

Just hours after Liao casts the poem "Massacre" into the air, its prophecy comes true. The People's Liberation Army opens fire on the crowd, killing hundreds. It will become known as the Tiananmen Square massacre. Liao makes only a few recorded copies of the poem, but it catches on, and more are bootlegged and disseminated, and soon half of China hears it. The poet is quickly arrested and given a prison sentence of four years. And then the torture begins. They beat him, starve him, and prod his anus with electric rods, and on one occasion chopsticks. All of this because of the simple act of documenting in poetry what might happen, what was happening, and what had already happened. And then, as a final act of condemnation, they take away Liao's only weapons—his pencil and paper. With nothing to write on, he becomes a devout listener. He listens to the stories of the men who share his fate, prisoners, the invisible people of society, from all regions in China, from all backgrounds and traditions. They are there, and they have stories. And Liao cannot write any of this down. He cannot record or document any of it. So he shape-shifts. His ears become audio recorders, his heart a steno pad. He prompts stories from these prisoners, time and again, the same stories. And soon he commits them to memory. Years pass, and finally the poet is released from prison. He gets busy putting down in writing the remembered stories of his fellow prisoners and comrades. To find a publisher he must smuggle the document out of China. Years after it was written, the book is finally released under the title *Interviews with People from the Bottom Rung of Society*. Here in the United States it's given the inconspicuous title *The Corpse Walker*.

It's a curious phenomenon the way certain people, or stories, or even songs exist in the world years before you come upon them, and the moment your life is positioned just so and the conditions align, and perhaps when you need them most, they suddenly appear on your radar. By the time I had learned of Liao Yiwu's story, I was in need of it. Without my realizing it, not only had a large part of my informal training come by way of my family, but all along, on the other side of that journey, there were stories and people making their way toward me. Not only were my blood ancestors guiding me, but so were a cadre of Storykeepers, witnesses, like Liao Yiwu, who had traversed the invisible road between where I stood and where they had already been. Some would become more critical to my journey than others.

ᘓ

When I first met the poet Juan Felipe Herrera and his wife Margarita Luna Robles, it was late spring of 1995, and the wound from losing Virgil was still a gash without scab. Juan Felipe was that stranger who first pointed at my journal writings and called them *poetry.* I was shocked to hear it. They brought me into their home on El Paso Street, in north Fresno, and treated me like a member of their family. Until then, I had been staying with friends, sleeping on couches, selling my paintings on the streets, and getting stoned daily. I wasn't a student at Fresno State, where he was teaching in those years. He would often ask me why I didn't enroll, and I'd just shrug and mumble something about grades. The truth is, I was waiting for a miracle. He and Margarita wanted to know what I was doing, what my plan was, besides staying numb. They sensed I was running from Visalia. They knew about Virgil. Over a span of a few years, they let me take refuge there, among their bookshelves and in the crease of their couch. They fed me poetry, ideas, and lasagna. I was exposed to a new world. Something in me had shattered, and the pieces were now being sutured back differently. I slept a lot, and mostly read. *I live to the rhythm of my country, and I cannot remain on the sidelines. I want to be here. I want to be part of it. I want to be a witness . . .* These words by Elena Poniatowska had found me one day. They were an invitation. And then there was Federico García Lorca's fire: *I denounce everyone who ignores the other half, the half that can't be redeemed, who lift their mountains of cement where the hearts beat . . .* Why had no one ever told me that poetry was built of the same rage I held within? These were the words I was looking for. They reflected back the pain that had been building up inside me since Virgil's death. Later, Rubén Martínez's *The Other Side* fell off the shelf and into my hands, and I was swept into new possibilities of what it meant *to search.* Juan Felipe and Margarita's private library became my hermitage; performance artists, muralists, anthropologists, I would do nothing for days but meld into the furniture of their study and make myself invisible. Sometimes Juan Felipe and I took walks, or had writing/art/clowning sessions, or sometimes we all dressed in costumes and goofed around in their living room—free expression, stories, tenderness, all of it medicine, administered to me daily. The wound was closing, and the light crept back in. Stories became the medicine. But also, my shield. I wanted more. I needed more. And then came one story in particular that would plant a most vital seed.

Juan Felipe told me about the time he was an undergraduate student at UCLA, in the early '70s, and he got a grant to trek into the Lacandón jungle and document the dwindling Maya population. He'd heard from an anthropology professor that their numbers were rapidly decreasing, and he needed to see for himself. He described to me in wonderful detail the things he'd seen and the friends he'd made, and how much that early trip shaped the view of his place in the world. How much it infused what poetry and community and his own familial past now meant to him.

He told me how he had gone searching for the Swiss anthropologist Trudi Blom, who spent decades chronicling the Maya in Chiapas. He talked to me about how naïve he was, only twenty-one years old, when he set out on that first trek, carrying bags of equipment and rolls of film that he would later abandon along the way. He shared with me the vulnerable ethics of entering space as an outsider and creating original ideas in the name of "documentation" or "art." *My trick lens signaled my privileged ground,* he would later write of the experience. All of this appealed to me, and at the time I didn't know why. The desire to go searching for my own meaning was planted. And to further solidify this, he handed me a VHS cassette that contained the raw footage of his first trek to Chiapas. Shots from the window of the small twin-engine Cessna floating down into the jungle foliage. And then silent footage of the Maya themselves, in canoes, or walking, or just standing in a milpa. He knew them all by name. Remembered them clearly. He considered them family.

"You have to go down there, Timeaus, see for yourself. Yes, that's coming up for you."

And he'd smile his wide smile, and I'd nod as if I actually believed it was possible. Though I knew it wasn't. Not in the broken state I was in. Not at that moment.

A year later he would go on to publish a book about his experiences in Chiapas, *Mayan Drifter: A Chicano Poet in the Lowlands of America.* He gifted me a copy, and that book became a bible to me. If there's one book written for every person on this planet, that one was mine. For years I wouldn't part with it.

Doors had opened. I walked through.

@

It was after dinner one evening that Juan Felipe sat me down at his dining room table and pulled out a giant poster board and colorful markers. He said, "Here's the plan for you. The road map." He drew a neon pink circle in the center of the poster. Inside of it he wrote, *Home.* Around the circle he drew a large five-pointed star. At the tip of each point he wrote the name of a different city and different goal. San Francisco—murals. Los Angeles—performance. Colorado—writing school. And so on. And each time he'd write another city he'd say, "But in between these you have to come home to see your parents." So from the center I would go out, meet the goal, then return home, start again from the center, out, then return. Until all five points of the star had been achieved. In that moment, standing in the thick of my own grief, I found his colorful map amusing, as if any of those things could actually be attained. It felt hopeless. He folded the giant poster up and handed it to me. "Stick it in your pocket," he said, jokingly. It wasn't until two decades later that I would come to realize that, deliberately or not, I had followed Juan Felipe's star-map almost to a T. Over the years, I had lived in those exact cities, accomplished the goal, and, just like he instructed, always returned home.

It was Juan Felipe's star-map that pointed me to Naropa University in Boulder, Colorado. A college founded on Buddhist principles. It housed a writing program known as the Jack Kerouac School of Disembodied Poetics, for the Beat authors who founded the program, many of whom still taught there. While there, we'd spend most days in meditation with the intention of cultivating a broader sense of awareness. Which is to say, we were learning the ancient practice of paying attention. I immersed myself in my studies and would soon learn the names of those who'd come before me seeking the same. It was there I'd learn of people like Harry Everett

Smith, an eccentric and somewhat mythical presence at Naropa. He had passed away by the time I arrived, but his stories remained. In audio and film, Harry documented everything and anything that caught his eye—from insects crawling across a wooden floor, to punk-rock bands in places like CBGB, to conversations at the kitchen tables of poets. His ability to pay attention was legendary. I became obsessed by the idea of cataloguing sound. It was under his influence that I would stick my audio recorder out onto the balcony of our home in Boulder, Colorado, and capture the wind whistling down from the Rocky Mountains. In the background you can hear Rumi, who was still an infant at the time, attempting to form language in her mouth. I was practicing.

Much later, I would learn about the mystical ethnographic work of the artist Quintan Ana Wikswo, and the windows of possibility would be forever slammed open. Wikswo scouts locations across the country where some form of grief or trauma has occurred. She camps there, alone, sometimes for days, and records the ambience of the space. As a kind of portal into the grief, she utilizes recording equipment that is of the time period in which the incident occurred. For instance, a house that once doubled as an underground abortion clinic in the year 1976 would require an audio recorder or camera used in 1976. Whereas Harry Smith was capturing the here and now, Quintan Ana Wikswo documents the spiritual and psychological realm of what once was.

And there were others I'd come to learn about who were doing this kind of work. There was the father-son team of John and Alan Lomax, who traveled across the United States in the 1930s recording the songs and stories of folks in black and immigrant communities otherwise unheard in those years. What a dream job, I would think to myself. To go around recording people's stories and songs in places I'd never think to pay attention to. And then there was Dorothea Lange. Having grown up in Tulare County, where a large population of Dust Bowl "Okies" had settled and made a life, her name was ubiquitous. But what struck me was not her photographs of migrant workers so much as the field notes she wrote on the backs of her photos. I was intrigued by the unseen narrative. Brief stories of the people and places captured in her lens. They were scribbled documentations of her witness, which I could not help but read as undelivered letters to an anonymous seeker in the future. Perhaps I was that seeker? And these researchers, or searchers, weren't relegated to any one region or place;

they were from everywhere. There was Maggie Nelson, who investigated her aunt Jane's death and wrote *The Red Parts,* and similarly Mark Arax, the Fresno journalist who used his investigative skills to find the people responsible for his father's murder. Some personal, some political. Some both. The reasons varied. But what they had in common was that each one was called by their subject for a purpose only they understood. But my own purpose was still unclear. I was in pursuit of what they had already come to discover for themselves—the source of what was calling me, and why. I was relentless. I sought out more books. More names. And because harvesting is in my DNA, I began gathering quotes and excerpts from all of them. People who had done the work. I toted their words around, in my head, in my cell phone, and in my journals, sometimes as talismans, sometimes as keys. They became a chorus of voices, and also my accompaniment on the loneliest stretches of living.

While traveling throughout Mexico during that first search, each time I heard don Leovardo say to me, "El recordar es vivir," I could hear Studs Terkel echo back, "In their rememberings are their truths." Or when don Miguel told me the fantastical story of the prehistoric horse, I could see Charles Bowden squinting his eyes in the desert sunlight, saying, "I believe in many things that may not have happened, and I do not believe in many things that have happened." Or when I first went to the crash site and there on the fence was a sign that said No Trespassing, I heard Woody Guthrie's lyrics ring out, "But on the other it doesn't say nothin' / that side was made for you and me." It was all the permission I needed. These are the conversations I've held in my head since I first began searching for people, starting with Bea Franco in 2008. It continues. Collectively, I hear their voices counseling me along the way, assuaging all doubt when the search grows dim or the trail cold and I feel like throwing up my hands and quitting. This chorus is made of voices—tender, hardened, wise, humorous, defiant voices, some gone, many still with us: bell hooks, Rebecca Solnit, Zora Neale Hurston, Eduardo Galeano, Cristina Rivera Garza, Luis Alberto Urrea, Joan Didion, Truman Capote, Alfredo Corchado, Susan Griffin, Stephanie Elizondo Griest, Héctor Tobar, Jonathan Safran Foer, Terry Tempest Williams, and countless others. These are just a few of the names.

This is what it comes down to, what I've learned from each of them. With or without our knowing, we carry the spoken and silent hopes of those we surround ourselves with. Those we hear, and even those we pretend not to. We commonly refer to this as "inspiration," but it is more. Scholars might call this "dialogism," but we'll leave that for the classroom. Regardless of what name we give it, we are, all of us, engaged in a very alive conversation across time and geography, which is constant and without end. What we call it isn't important. What is important is that this too is the community. This too is the caracol. Every one of them a sturdy bridge, support in the broken spaces between one story and another, my story and yours. And they remind us that no matter where we are in our personal lives, the story we are meant to hear will find us when we are ready to receive it.

40

THE UNEARTHING OF APOLONIO PLASCENCIA RAMÍREZ

What you seek is seeking you.

—JALALUDDIN RUMI

August 24, 2020

I'M IN the early stages of putting together this manuscript when I receive a message on social media. A woman named Barbara Varela Plascencia writes:

Hi Tim! I'm writing from a tiny town south of Belgium, a country where I have lived for the past thirty plus years but born and raised in Mexico. I believe my uncle Apolonio Plascencia Ramírez is one of the 28 Los Gatos Canyon deportees. Thank you so much for your contribution to give them the dignity they deserve.

I'm skeptical. I try not to be. But after more than a decade of this work, I've learned a few things. If what Barbara tells me is true, this will make Apolonio passenger number twelve. I check her profile to learn more about her. The image she uses as her photo immediately captures my attention. It's a brushstroke painting of the Vietnamese Buddhist monk Thich Nhat Hanh. The image reads: *No Mud, No Lotus.* I know this quote well. A year ago, I painted a portrait of him with that very quote on it. It's been hanging in my living room ever since. I take it as a sign. I reply:

Barbara, I would really like to speak with you. I've been looking for Apolonio's family. Is there a number I can reach you at? And is there a good day/time for you?

We arrange to speak by phone a few days later. But the very next day, excited about the discovery, she sends me another email:

Dear Tim, I'm still flabbergasted and in the process of getting more information about my uncle. In the meantime, please find attached this photo. Circa 1952, you will see Apolonio's siblings: Alejandro (brother), Aída (sister), María (sister / my mum), Rosalva Varela (my sister, deceased). Children: Miguel Ángel Reyes (nephew), Óscar Nieto (nephew), Nacho Varela (my brother—Apolonio's nephew). Kneeling/sitting, Guadalupe (sister) and Bárbara Ramírez (my grandmother and Apolonio's mum). I think you mentioned you already have his birth certificate. If not, please let me know and I'll send it to you. I'm also trying to get a hold of your book! Échale un ojo ;) Take care!

Once a photograph is sent to me, things change. People are invoked. And if you sit with the image for a moment, without too much overthinking, you can feel them staring at you.

I search the faces. None of which are Apolonio. By the time this photo is taken he is four years dead. His mother is here, Bárbara Ramírez. She's kneeling before a basket. Next to her is Apolonio's sister, Guadalupe. Behind them, a row of nieces and nephews. And standing behind the children are the rest of Apolonio's siblings. He's the only one missing from this photo. And the empty shoes, front and center, call attention to the absence. The shoes are not positioned right side up. They're face down, toward the earth. Side by side. As if placed there deliberately. And yet no one is barefoot. Only they know why.

Apolonio's family, Guadalajara, Jalisco, circa 1952.

41

THE TESTIMONY OF BARBARA VARELA PLASCENCIA

I HAD INITIALLY felt that Apolonio's story was still too recent a discovery to include in this book. Typically, I wait until enough information comes forth about the passenger before including their story. I've learned that time alone reveals more information than any amount of investigative probing. But the conversations I had with Barbara Varela Plascencia over the next couple of years were far different from any of the others I'd had so far, and for that reason I felt they needed to be considered. Too, it seemed her own experiences were aligned with my personal situation and my contemplations about family and spirituality, and many times during our phone calls I felt as if I alone was the intended audience for her stories. As if I was *meant* to hear them.

What struck me first about Barbara's perspective was that she chose a life for herself and her children far outside of either Mexico or the United States. I know firsthand the hard decision to raise children away from all that is familiar and comfortable, and without the support of family. It's a gamble that you pray will somehow pay off in the end. Also, I found it unique that her perspective was removed from the codependency between the two countries. Initially, the bulk of our conversations were mostly by email, and sometimes through social media, but more recently they occurred by phone. The time difference was always a factor. As she was waking up, I was already going to sleep. The result was a conversation in stops and starts. For this reason, I've had to suture our conversations together. But to read these fragments is to glimpse the far-reaching impact Apolonio's death had on his family, even just one generation removed. Not from someone who stood on one side or the other of the U.S.-Mexico border, but from someone who stood at a completely different vantage point. And sometimes, perspective alone is reason enough to leave home.

੦

Barbara: "Well, I live here in Belgium. I've been living here for thirty-plus years now, but I'm originally from Mexico City. My family moved there from Los Altos de Jalisco in the '40s. I didn't have a chance to meet my uncle Apolonio, but I always mutter a little prayer to him whenever I take a plane. And, well, this has been a story that's been going through my head since I was a child. It was a sad story in the family, of course. My mother, Apolonio's sister, would get very sad when she'd tell it to us.

"I'll just . . . let me start again. I'm the niece of Apolonio Plascencia Ramírez, he was my uncle. My mother is Apolonio's sister, her name was María Plascencia Ramírez. My tío had four siblings; he was the middle child. My grandfather's name was Ramón Plascencia, and my grandmother was Bárbara Ramírez. My mother named me after her mother. [*Pause.*] To be honest, I only know that my uncle had left for the United States with his father Ramón. They both went legally, as braceros. And I remember my mother saying something about them being in Oakland, California, and I understand there was a fight in a bar and the police came, and they raided the bar but only took the Mexicans. They put them in a bus, and then the plane, y bombedas! That's it. Just like they do now, I guess. Despite the fact that they had papers and were in the U.S. legally, my uncle was deported. His father Ramón wasn't on the plane. My grandmother didn't learn about the accident right away. She never recovered his . . . she didn't get his remains back. She only got a plastic bag with some of his belongings. That must've been so heartbreaking. Can you imagine for a mother to just . . . he was very young when the crash happened. She just got this bag of his stuff, a watch, a pair of cufflinks, things he was carrying. Apolonio's father often worked in the United States as a bracero. He'd done that more than once, as I understand. And he, uh . . . he even had a gringa mistress. He would come back home to San Miguel el Alto every year, just long enough to leave my grandmother pregnant. And he did that every year, and by the fifth year my grandmother Bárbara learned about the mistress and so she [*laughs*], she greeted my grandfather at the door with a gun in her hand. And she told him, 'You're not welcome anymore.' So that's when my grandfather went back to the States. My grandma sold everything she had and migrated to Mexico City. The family spread out after that. I have photos of the family, of Apolonio's brothers and sisters, and of my grandparents too. But we have never found one of Apolonio yet, unfortunately."

How did you end up in Belgium?

"I was just twenty-one, recently divorced and with a baby. I was still living in Mexico, working for the 1986 World Cup organization, and I met this Belgian man, with blue eyes. He was working for a European television network. We met, and went out, and that was pretty much how it happened. When I first arrived here, thirty-five years ago, I didn't speak any French or Dutch. I cleaned houses to get money and I had no papers at the time, so I did babysitting, etc. When I first came here there were quite a few Mexican women married to Belgians. Mexican wives were well regarded because they were considered 'good mothers' and 'obedient.' Eventually there was an opening for an office job at the Mexican embassy, so I worked there for many years, and then later went on to other international institutions."

Aside from the "few wives," were there any other Mexicans in Belgium when you arrived?

"There's a small Mexican community, mainly in Brussels and in the Flemish part of the country. But back then it was mainly composed of what I guess you would call 'souvenir wives.' At the time Alcatel, a huge Belgian company, had operations in Veracruz, Mexico. So whenever a Belgian engineer who was single went to work there, he usually came back married to a 'linda jarocha.' And there were other opportunities, like the Olympic Games in 1968, and the World Cup in 1970 and 1986. So then a new wave of young people began arriving: IT experts, engineers, artists. Also, several Mexican priests attended the famous theology chair at the Catholic University of Leuven. And some of them would stay to attend to parishes, in view of the dire shortage of local priests. But for the most part, Mexicanos here are still regarded as exotic, or funny and harmless. To them we are still located 'somewhere in South America.' Belgians typically don't know much about Mexico. They still say stuff like, 'Oh, you're from Mexico? I have an Argentinian friend, you should meet her.'"

You mentioned you had once been deported while living there?

"In Belgium, as in other European countries, everyone has an identity card, and you have to establish a house address. And since I had no papers at the time, I received a letter saying I had ten days to leave the country. I was really sad about it at the time. You feel like, well, you're a human being, and you know you have a right to pursue your own happiness, but, uh . . . I was worried for my little girl. She was already enrolled in kindergarten, and I was just so sad at the time. I had no money for the trip. I was cleaning this lady's house and she was kind enough to pay for my plane ticket to leave the country. After the ten days are up they send the police to see if you're still living there, and they ask the neighbors too.

"As soon as I got back to Mexico I knew I needed to return to Belgium. In my case, there was a love story. And also, I had my little girl, and I wanted a better life for her. So my husband, who was my fiancé at the time, decided to try and get me there on a student visa. He enrolled me in college and took care of the financial part so that I could come back. Meanwhile, I kept visiting the Belgian embassy in Mexico City, and . . . well, I'm very bad at lying, and I was talking to the consul there, and I told her I wanted to get back to attend school. And she said, 'Why do you want to go back right now if classes start in September?' I couldn't lie, I just told her, 'I'm missing my fiancé.' And the consulate woman sped up the process for me. It was like that back then. But times are much different now. I think of people from Afghanistan and Syria, seeking a better life, sleeping in the cold, in the forest, it's just so unfair. I think a lot about my uncle Apolonio, who was working, creating wealth for the United States, and contributing to the economy, and I find it unfair that, uh, children who are absolutely innocent are living in such horrible conditions. They're innocent, they have no role in any of this, and yet they're dying.

"You know, after my grandma Bárbara was left alone with her five children, they were very, very poor. And Apolonio was one of those children. And when he was old enough he went to the States to work with his father. They were so poor they couldn't afford shoes or underwear. Nowadays I look at my daughter, and she's made a good life for herself, and I'm so proud of what she's achieved. And, well, my grandchildren don't speak Spanish, but my eldest grandson, he's nine. He was recently telling me that at his school there are gangs, like the Polish gang, the Italian gang, and the French-speaking gang. And I asked him, 'What gang are you with?' And he told me, 'I'm in the Mexican gang, and I'm alone because I'm the only Mexican.' [*Laughs.*]"

I'm curious, why the Thich Nhat Hanh quote on your social media page?

"Ah, yes. Well, growing up I was raised Catholic, very devout. I went to Catholic school, where they teach you the worst parts, sin and the devil and punishment, and, well, not a very nice experience. So, when I arrived here, I was very lonely initially. And I was telling a doctor how lonely I was, and how I had no friends. And he told me that there was this vegetarian restaurant here where people will just talk with you, you should try it. So I would go there and have tea, and people were kind, and began talking to me. And there is where I discovered a course, Introduction to Tibetan Buddhism, and so I went. And it was like, wow, like just, you find that that's what this is all about, no sin, no hell, no heaven. It was all about liberation. And I suddenly understood so many things. That was back in 1995. Nowadays I say I'm a Buddhist devoted to la Virgen de Guadalupe. I could be a better Buddhist, but I don't lose hope of one day becoming a good practitioner.

"You know, my mother, she was very, well, just very sad about her brother. Very sad. And I believe I inherited my mother's sadness. But not only that, I also inherited her struggle to stay alive, and also, I mean, all the violence. There used to be a lot of violence in our family, and I can feel [*pauses*] . . . I still feel that. But I take pride in saying that the violence stops with me now. And that this sadness stops with me. Nowadays I write, I volunteer with patient organizations, I study theater at the conservatory, and I even started singing. And when I look at my own daughter, and my five grandchildren . . . I can see the light in them. Such light. And I know that I'm the last one in my family who will ever carry this burden. It all stops with me. I believe this. And I truly believe that it's not a coincidence that you and I found each other. I believe there's a reason for all of this."

42

VIRGIL AS RELIQUARY

1995

MONTHS AFTER Virgil is killed, my mom gives me some of his belongings. A manila envelope with documents: the police report, his wallet, a notebook, a wedding band, a restraining order, and dozens of keys. These are just some of the clues. I sort through them, not really reading so much as scanning. I still haven't accepted that he's gone. Not yet. She tells me that I can have his chest. Some days I'll spend hours in the garage, alone, with his chest flung open, holding what I can of him. His leather work belt still carries his tools. A flat carpenter's pencil, a snap line with red chalk spilling out, a pocket of framing nails. I pull his hammer from the holster, grip its handle, and I can almost feel the warmth from his hand there. I smell the handle for the scent of his sweat. I need to know that he was once alive, that he existed. This is what I'm searching for. I long to feel him still. When Virgil walked this earth there was a part of the world I didn't have to concern myself with because he existed in that part, and he was holding that part up for me, for all of us.

Sometimes in a family, one person is appointed to have all the feelings for everyone. And sometimes, one person is required to have none. This is an excerpt from work by the investigative artist Quintan Ana Wikswo. I have committed it to memory. I often ask myself which one Virgil was. And then one day it occurs to me. He was the one appointed to have all the feelings, though he tried hard to be the one that didn't. By default, he had become our family's reliquary.

I'll keep his chest close to me, every few days return to it, dig through, looking for hints of the man I love, despite his flaws. It dawns on me now that it was for his flaws that I had come to idolize my uncle. It was easy for me to see through his rough exterior, to the small boy who had grown up an orphan under difficult circumstances. It was easy for me because I had learned the stories of our family. My mom made sure I would not forget them. In this way too, Virgil was my first foray into what compassion felt like. And it was reciprocal because I knew that he never judged me either. He didn't need to. This is the privilege of the uncle. And perhaps that fact alone is what I was drawn to. That he was the most nonjudgmental witness of my life.

ര

His truck is still parked on the side of our house. I sit in the driver's seat, grip the steering wheel, look out the windshield, through Virgil's eyes. Imagine him driving to where he would soon be killed. I recall a few conversations we had in his truck. How I once lent him my favorite coffee mug, and it rolled off his seat and shattered on the floorboard. I hear him—

"Goddamn, sorry about that, mijo. I'll get you a new one."

We talk about women, and the news. Selena, the Tex-Mex icon, has just been killed.

"What a fucking loss," he says.

O. J. Simpson gets away with it.

"Money'll buy you anything."

He shakes his head. We laugh. Sitting there with him, I begin to cry. I forage through the glove box, wedge my hand between his seats. He asks me what I'm searching for.

"I don't know," I say.

I just know that something compels me to stick my hand into the particulars of his life.

"I'm looking for evidence," I say, half joking.

"Be careful," he says, "you might find what you're looking for."

I honestly don't know what I'm searching for. I trust I'll know when I find it. Maybe clues to what brought him to die in such a way. Maybe

I'm searching for a new understanding. Or the right words. There are a hundred ways I could've pictured my uncle dying, but not the way he did. It's true, he had long since told himself a story, a story about fatherhood, and how it all ends. A story he had lived as a child. A story impressed upon him by his own father, Alejandro. And now it was his turn to pass back through again, this time in the role of father. He had attempted to change the narrative and paid the price for it. But was there dignity in his death? I need to know. How could there have been, when he was afforded such little dignity in his life? I may never find the answers I'm searching for. Certainly not here in his truck, among the crushed beer cans and spent sunflower seeds. Not in his chest. Not in memory. Not anywhere.

ര

In the mid-'90s the Visalia Police Department was under scrutiny because they were killing unarmed men of color at a high rate. The circumstances always questionable. Immediately after Virgil's death, local news channels came to our home seeking an interview. I don't recall what exactly they asked, but I do remember what I said into the camera. "He was loved." That's it. I was sure no one was watching on the other end. No one was paying attention. I repeated again and again, "He was loved. He was loved." It was all I could say. I was aware of how inarticulate I was. But I hadn't the words. Neither did my parents. I just needed the people responsible for his death to know that they had killed a loved man. At the time, I believed that the reason the police were able to coldly kill my uncle was because they could not see this fact. Not because they had calloused hearts, but because between their heart and their ability to see an anonymous brown man as someone worthy of love was a certain kind of wall. A border. Virgil was the latest incarnation of Ellison's "invisible man." They could not see his face through the living-room window at night. They could not look into his eyes, and they did not know his story. They didn't know that beyond the limit of their imagination was a father who desperately loved his son and was reacting to his own fear rooted in having already lost a son once before. They could not possibly imagine an anonymous brown man containing such softness within him. No. As far as they were concerned, the nameless man who barricaded himself in with the little boy was a phantom, not of flesh and bone, but of discardable material. I cannot write the word "matter" because it didn't. And because he was a phantom, he did not merit the dignity or respect only afforded to the visible ones. A judgment was made.

Attorneys contacted us with talk of a class-action lawsuit. They wanted us to meet with another family, that of a man who was shot out of a tree, also unarmed. A few months prior, in the nearby town of Dinuba, where I was born, a Mexican grandfather, a farmworker, was dragged out of bed by the cops in the middle of the night and killed. A case of "mistaken identity." All around me invisible people were being killed, and they just so happened to look like me and my family. Something I was no stranger to by now. I was twenty-one years old, but the tremors that had been planted in me as a teenage boy would all come rushing back to find me. I became afraid of everything. And because I was afraid I needed desperately to control my environment and anyone inside of it. I learned it had a name. Anxiety. It was fear that looked more like a need for control but manifested as anger. I was pissed off. And I began to see cops, and all authority, through the same one-dimensional lens through which they saw me. A shiny badge was a clear threat to my existence. Strike that. Let me be real. Anything and anyone I could not control posed a threat to my existence, including people I loved. And I began acting out in toxic and hurtful ways.

I wondered when my parents would begin the process of investigation. When they'd seek justice. Days passed. And then months. It was infuriating. I would never hear talk of it. We just sat there, pathetic, in the fog of our grief. We were failing. I was failing. Not only did it rob us of our will to move on, but, more importantly, it stripped us of our voices. We'd become silent. Even with each other. No words seemed to fit. The questions piled up. I grew angrier with the passing of each day. More brown men were killed in our hometown. Community vigils came and went. Highways got named after slain police officers. Meanwhile, Virgil's death was old news. Swept under the walnut groves and rows of grapes. I felt wordless and stupid. I took it out on anyone within arm's reach. A wrath took root. We would never be seen. Never be heard. Virgil would never get justice. We would forever remain fucking invisible. Silenced indefinitely. You want to know how it all got started? Where it all began? I would say here. This. This was the beginning.

43

METHODOLOGY OF GHOSTS

The chronicles that comprise this book record
a search for the home that I've lost and found
countless times. . . . It has been, it is, in other words,
a search for a one that is much more than two.
—RUBÉN MARTÍNEZ, *THE OTHER SIDE / EL OTRO LADO*

WORDS. I want to know the full potential of their power. And their inherent weakness. To get there we must begin with their origins. I look up the etymology for *search.* From Old French, *cercher.* To seek out. And Old Latin *circus,* meaning "circle." To return back to. What does it mean for me that I seek out and return back to, again and again? I leave a home and return to a new home, and still find both places empty of who I was before. "How's the search going?" people ask, surprised that I've sustained this for thirteen years and counting. I'm never sure how to reply. If I offer them the math, maybe it would all make sense. I wonder, if I were to say, "Six thousand hours and $30,000, that's how it's going," would it elicit a different response beyond the typical nod? At a family gathering my tía Dolores asks me, "Mijo, who pays you to do this?"

"No one," I reply. She stares at me, waiting for the punchline. I add, "God, I guess." She chuckles. No one wants to hear the particulars of what the actual work entails. The questions are veiled. When people ask, "How's the search going?" what they really want are the stories.

I offer this:

I bought my children a jeweler's loupe once and we spent the day staring through it, investigating our everyday surroundings. We'd press the loupe against a tree trunk, into the dirt, or against our skin, in total awe of just how much was happening beneath the surface, if we paid close enough attention. Everything we took for granted was suddenly imbued with meaning. A simple loupe.

Here's another:

A woman lives in a neighborhood from the time she is young. She calls it home for the majority of her life. For decades she tends to the place, the people, and even the stray animals. The neighborhood itself sits on the edge of El Paso, just yards away from the borderline. Its history goes back to the days of the Mexican Revolution. But now the woman is in her nineties and the buildings are decrepit, and the city wants to tear it all down to build a sports arena. They pay the residents to leave, and most accept the offer, except for the woman. They try other tactics too, but she doubles down. She's made her stance clear. She isn't going anywhere. Soon the media catches wind. The *New York Times*, the *L.A. Times*, they all write articles about this elderly fronteriza who refuses to bend to gentrification and takes a stand for history. Toñita Morales, they say, is the "Protector of Barrio Duranguito." Artists paint her image on walls, her fist raised, in defiance. She waits and waits, until finally she wins. History wins. Now she is a local hero. And, as I have only recently come to learn, my blood relative. A first cousin of my grandmother Magdalena—Chita's mother. And she lives less than a mile away from me. Why, after nine years of living in El Paso, am I just now learning that Toñita Morales and I share blood?

Search. Cercher. Circus.

I'm only now coming to understand something most crucial. If I'm to look at this work honestly, all these years of searching have produced very little. Read the stories again. In almost every case, the families have found *me*. They have admitted to seeking *me* out. All I have done is set the intention.

When I was still an undergraduate at Naropa, I once had the privilege of sitting down to dinner with Alice Walker, the legendary peace activist and author of *The Color Purple*. There were only a few of us students present.

It was a two-hour occasion and one of the highlights of my life. Yet I can only remember one thing that was said that night. Someone commented to Alice that she must "devour books" in her spare time. To which she very nonchalantly replied, "No, actually. I spend most of my time trying to clear my mind so that I can see when that next great story comes along." It is always about paying attention.

In our working-class family, it seemed we only had two gears that we toggled between—drive and reverse, the past and the future. To be present is a privilege not afforded to the struggling class. Our parents encouraged us to chase our dreams, but we were never taught what to do once we achieved them. They never prepared us how to *be* inside the dream. Or how to recognize when we're even standing *in* the dream. This is because no one we knew had ever attained it. Whatever *it* was. And even now, as I sit behind my cozy desk on the fifth floor of a university that overlooks two countries, I find it nearly impossible to remain present. The two-headed serpent of hindsight and foresight has been coded in my DNA for generations—a condition not even four years at a Buddhist college, which required endless hours of meditation, was able to reprogram. I feel like Janus, the mythological Roman god resigned to eternally looking forward and backward. This Janusian curse is my inheritance. I have to practice moderation toward that great pastime of my ancestors, longing and dreaming.

A few years ago, at our family's annual Fourth of July barbecue, I was sitting in a lawn chair next to my uncle Joe. It was night out, the sky was clear, and because we were outside the city limits, it was wonderfully dark. I pointed up at the sky and told my uncle, "Check out the stars, tío, they're so bright tonight." He looked up and for several long minutes silently marveled at what he was seeing. He eventually turned to me and whispered, "Mijo, do you know how long it's been since I've looked at the stars?"

44

A REMEMBERED CONVERSATION WITH MY THERAPIST

2018

—You are not your history, Tim. Our ego hangs on to things like this, which we call our identity. Because without it what are you, right? It's helpful to let go of the past.

—I realize that, but the problem is that parts of our history have been erased. How am I supposed to care about history while letting go of it? I don't know how to reconcile the two.

—What you're doing has value, of course. And humans are blessed with memory, it's the material we're made of. What I'm saying is that the label of "historian" is only an invention of the ego. You've made this your sense of identity. Being the keeper of the past, or "the Storykeeper," as you call it, is the identity *you've* created. Not just the plane crash story, but with your family's history, your cultural history, all sorts of histories. And that's a whole lot of luggage to carry around, isn't it? None of that is you. It's only the material that made you, but you are not those series of events. Just like wood and nails can make a house, but the house serves its own purpose. A house stops being a house the moment a family moves in. It transforms into a home. Does this make sense?

—I think so. But what does this mean, then, for me and the work I'm doing? Should I stop?

—Does it bring you joy? Fulfillment?

—I wouldn't call it joy. But it makes me feel like I'm getting closer to something.

—What do you mean?

—I don't know. I keep trying to figure it out, but it gets away from me. I can't describe it. Every time a new family comes to me it's like I finally put a face to the name and the soul that I'd been wondering about for years. People whom I don't know, but who've lived inside of me for so long. People I've thought about and even care about, but they're faceless and bodyless. And when I do finally meet them and see their faces or shake their hand it feels like . . . like such a relief, like my soul can breathe again. I know this sounds dramatic, but it's the only way I can describe it.

Silence.

—Do you think that maybe the abortions have something to do with that feeling?

—What do you mean?

—Well, you told me that being a part of the abortion process at two different times in your life was a guilt you've always carried with you. Do you think this search, the way you go about trying to find people that you don't know, hoping to put a face to these anonymous souls, is maybe your way of trying to redeem yourself? Maybe by finding these people you're healing something inside of you?

Silence.

—I'd never thought about that before. Like restoring my karma?

—Sure, you can put it that way. Or just trying to . . . well, alleviate that void.

—I honestly never considered that. Guess I've always felt like Rumi and Sal were my redemption. I've always believed they were the same two souls that returned, giving me a second chance.

—And they are, Tim. But they are in your present moment. They are in your *right now.* Not in your past. Since they were born have you thought much about the abortions?

—No, not really. Not anymore.

—Well, that's good. That's what I'm saying here. You see, in that instance, you aren't allowing history to determine the kind of father you are in the present. Stay there, Tim. That's a good place to be.

45

THE BUTTERFLY

MOM CORRECTS ME. It was Roel's death that she had witnessed her father Alejandro making a coffin for. "And it didn't happen in Socorro, New Mexico," she says. "It happened in Roma, Texas." She has just finished reading a draft of these stories. "You confused the two. I don't blame you, a lot of babies died." She explains, "Tillie (one) was first, and then later, in Socorro, Betito passed. Then Roel. And then much later, Tilly (two). Virgil was the last one."

By the time Magdalena died of cancer, Alejandro had buried three of his children, and then his wife. I've been told these stories since as far back as I can remember, and yet my memory did not retain the details. Because history must be willing to revise itself, I make the necessary changes. What I held on to most over the years was the unresolved grief that was transferred in the telling. These stories would shape me in more ways than I'll ever understand.

As a kid, the butterfly omen fascinated me more than any other story. Such seemingly harmless creatures. It was the one detail I did hang on to. I eventually came to reason: if the butterfly was the harbinger of all the deaths in my family, including my grandmother's, then it was also responsible for my mother's suffering. Growing up, I witnessed the effects of her grief manifested as anger, and often felt the curse was still looming in our lives. Her fire, at times, destroyed things—objects, yes, but also our sense of safety. As a teenager I grew to match her energy and rebelled against her authority. I tested it often, and often I failed. I recall one vicious argument in the hallway, the same hallway where we received the news of Virgil's death. I was being disrespectful, and she stepped toward me, so I dared her to slap me, and she did. I kept my face there and cussed at her, daring her to slap me again. And again she did. I spat again. And again a slap jolted me. She needed to unleash. And I needed to feel punished. This is the cycle. This is love. We went a few more rounds of this, until finally, both cheeks red and raw, I backed away. After I was arrested for drinking and driving, she took me on a long drive, which ended with both of us yelling at the top of our lungs at one another. I opened the door and threatened to jump. My mother pressed on the gas and sped the car up, and said, "If you're going to do it then do it!" She knew I didn't have it in me. After all, she had survived so much and yet somehow still managed to keep her heart open enough to love her children with abandon.

Let me rewrite that.

This is what I knew of love. It looked angry. It acted that way. It shouted and screamed. And then, later, after the silence became unbearable, it made amends. Sometimes with just a few words. Sometimes with more. I went about the world this way, calling it love.

But then there was this—

One day, during the month of December, my mom asks me to help her load a small Christmas tree, along with several wrapped gifts, into our car. We then drive sixteen miles to the small farming community of Cutler, a town where we had lived years ago. When we arrive, we pull up to a dilapidated concrete building. The doors and windows are boarded up, and it looks abandoned. From one opening, a long, pink cotton drape blows in the breeze. We get out of the car, and Mom calls out to see if anyone is there. A man's voice replies in Spanish, "Adelante!"

The man steps out from behind the drape, smiling. He greets my mom: "Señora Hernandez, cómo estás?" He invites us in. Mom and I grab the gifts from the car. We enter the space, which is a gutted building with broken concrete floors and no running water. It's a single room, with curtains for walls. We are instantly greeted by the man and his three giggly children. The children are young, no more than ten. They are ecstatic at the sight of gifts; they jump up and down, shove each other for a closer view. I set the tree down in the center of the room, and the man is smiling, thanking us profusely. It all happens in Spanish, but I understand most of it. He keeps bowing his head, saying, "Gracias, Señora Hernandez, gracias." My mom bows back, insists he please call her Lydia. The children tug at their father's shirt, and he tells them to thank "Señora Hernandez y su hijo," and they do. My mom bends down to comb the girl's hair with her fingers, and tells her the gifts are from Santa. Her little eyes light up. More than anything, it's the way my mom addresses the man and his children that I pay attention to. I would later learn the word for this is *dignity*. We say our goodbyes, wish them a happy holiday, and the children wave at us as we drive away. In the car we are silent. But not a moment later Mom bursts into tears. She sobs and sobs. As if she'd been holding it all in. I don't know what or why. I let her cry for several minutes without saying a word. Finally she gathers herself. She tells me, "Those babies watched their mama die of cancer just a month ago." She pauses. "I just saw my little brothers' and sisters' faces in those babies. I saw all of us as kids after Mom died." I can see her mind is replaying the images. I haven't the words. Not in this moment. We drive the rest of the way home in complete silence.

It occurs to me only now that perhaps Mom had come face-to-face with Chita again that day. And in that small exchange, as she was reaching back to love herself, the reflection of it undid the years of grief she'd been carrying. If this is true, then it stands to reason that grief is just an accumulation of love that's had nowhere to go for too long. And perhaps by giving that love away, paying it forward, the numbing silence we are left with afterward, that long quiet drive home, is where healing resides.

VIII

SOMETHING LIKE REDEMPTION

I do not see my life as separate from history.
In my mind my family secrets mingle with
the secrets of statesmen and bombers.

—SUSAN GRIFFIN, *A CHORUS OF STONES*

46

THEY

IN THE BEGINNING, I had no other name for them but *ghosts.* For the relentless way they arrived unannounced. Compromised by years of brokenness. The past. The wounds. This is just one lens through which to see them. A fractured lens. For thirteen years now I've been on an exhaustive and perpetual search for people I do not know. This is the story I've told myself. I've gone to the cities, ranchitos, towns, and countries, and have circled back to the archives, the sites of tragedy, and the cemeteries. I've asked all the questions, left all the offerings, broken bread with the families, and come to a new understanding of my purpose. All at their invitation. At their calling. And now I am circling back to the beginning. My beginning.

2021

I am told by my mother that somewhere in the shadow of New Mexico's Florida Mountains, where my grandmother Magdalena was born, lives a relative named Danny Maynes. He is "up in age" now, but he owns a large portion of the land there, where he has a small cabin that he's dedicated entirely to a family shrine—a generational altar, if you will. I am told that the shrine is made up of countless photos of our family, some that predate the Mexican Revolution. I'm also intrigued that we have relatives who've put roots down in the terrain of our ancestors.

I drive out to visit Danny, and after several wrong turns down dirt roads that are hidden beneath chaparral bushes, I find his place with the help of a cousin. It's exactly as it was described to me. A small mobile home in the middle of the desert. Danny is sitting beneath his wooden patio throwing back a few beers. He doesn't know who I am or why I'm there. I tell him that Magdalena, "Nena," was my grandmother, and that Alejandro was my grandfather. He nods, as if still trying to figure it out. I tell him "El Gusano" was my grandpa, and then he lightens up. "Oh, Goozy," he says, grinning. "That's what I know him by. Yes, I used to know your grandpa pretty well. Oh yeah, we would drink, and man, how he and your grandma loved to dance."

The image of it alone brings me to tears. "That's what I heard," I say. "They loved to dance."

For all the painful memories of my grandparents, I only ever want to remember them dancing.

"And I used to know your great-grandpa too, Manuel Corona Maynes. He was my tío. They called him El Tejano. He was a tall man, almost seven feet. He had these huge hands, he was a real cowboy. He worked at Nan Ranch, out by Silver City. Yeah, I remember him. In fact, I have a picture of him with his wife Nicolasa. Hold on—"

"Is this the photo?" I hand him my phone. He looks at it and nods.

"Yes, that's him." He pauses. Looks up at me, then back at the photo. "Shit, you even look like your great-grandpa!" I take the phone back and stare at it. "Look at that. You look just like him." I strain to see the resemblance.

In the photo, my great-grandpa towers over his wife, who has a defiant stare, as she poses with one hand on her hip. On the ground sits a baby, dressed in white, and her left hand is raised, inviting you in. No one knows who the baby is. But her stare is haunting. It was taken in Columbus, New Mexico, in 1912, just four years prior to Pancho Villa's raid on the town. I grew up hearing stories about how my family got mixed up with the Mexican Revolution, on both sides of the battle.

Danny tells me that our family is originally from Valle de Allende, in Chihuahua, but then later they moved to Palomas, eventually crossing the border into the town of Columbus. I tell him how in all the years I'd grown up, I'd never heard of where in Mexico our family was from.

"We've been disconnected so long," I said, "so many generations."

"Yeah, well, now you know. That's where our people are from." He sips his beer, then asks me if I want to take a ride. A minute later we're in his old jeep bouncing through the desert, across his land, heading in the direction of the mountain that each morning would greet my great-grandparents, El Tejano and Nicolasa, with the rising sun. Danny is smiling, one hand on the wheel, staring out across the tops of the mesquite trees. He points to the faraway distance, in the direction of Mexico. "See those three mountains? Those are las tres hermanas," he says, and instantly I'm drawn back to the time we came here searching for Virgil. I remember my uncle telling us then about those very mountains. He is with me.

"Over near the mountains is where Columbus is," Danny says. "That's where El Tejano and Nicolasa lived. The foundation of their adobe house is still there. He used to ride a horse everywhere. Well, in those days that's what they did. If someone got sick they would take days to come to Deming just to see a doctor." Danny quiets. "That was a long time ago." He sips his beer and circles the jeep back to his house.

"What do you remember about my grandma and grandpa?" I ask him.

He tilts his head.

"I remember your grandma Nena very well. She was tall, like her dad. And a tough woman."

This is something I've heard echoed by those who knew her. At a family barbecue, my mother's cousin Manny once told me of a time my grandmother beat a man unconscious, and then held his head to the train tracks and waited for the oncoming train. People had to drag her away from him. Apparently, that story is still a sore spot for some in these parts.

Danny continues, "After she died, I don't remember seeing your grandpa anymore. I think he moved away, or . . . I just can't remember what happened to him." He looks at me. "Do you know what ever happened to him? What happened to Goozy?"

"He died at the VA hospital in Tucson," I say.

He nods, sips his beer.

Back at Danny's house, we look at the photos of people that adorn the walls and altar. He tells me their names. Who they were, how they're related to me. Then he leaves me alone to go fetch another beer.

I stare at all their faces. They have invited me here. I'm sure of this. This is what they do. I'm convinced that, more than any other reason, this is what my years of searching have been about. Less about me seeking out names and stories of the anonymous dead, and more about them seeking me. Or perhaps we are seeking each other. The more I help connect them to their family, the more they connect me to mine. And I know they'll be with me now for as long as I live. Sometimes one at a time. Sometimes more. Sometimes they will arrive in the middle of the night. And sometimes they will take other forms: a landscape, a conversation, a butterfly, a photograph. With each opportunity, I am pulled again, to another time, another place. Always with their eyes on me, and their hand out, inviting me to return again. Back to the road. Back to the spaces of our origins. Farther back still. Back to who we were in our original form. *Back to the rapture of first love.*

My great-grandparents, Nicolasa Flores and Manuel Corona Maynes, Columbus, New Mexico, circa 1912.

47

THE CALIFORNIA STATE SENATE

Sacramento, California, January 29, 2018

I AM NOW standing in front of the State Capitol building in Sacramento. With me are the families of four of the plane crash victims—Jaime and Lilia Ramírez, Rosa María and her daughter Lisa, Ofelia Treviño and her daughter Ofelia—and my family. The survivors are carrying framed photos of their relatives who were killed in the plane crash at Los Gatos. They are: Francisco Durán Llamas, Guadalupe Ramírez Lara, Ramón Paredes González, and Tomás Márquez Padilla. We walk inside, past the metal detectors, into the halls of the fifth-largest state capitol in the United States. We know why we're here. We know what we represent. It's the first and only time in seventy years that this incident will be formally recognized by the government. Never once in this journey did I imagine we would be here. And certainly not at the invitation of politicians. There's a quiet nervousness in the air.

We cram into an elevator, all of us, more intimate than we've ever been. But it feels right. We can't help it, we suddenly burst into laughter. The closeness undoes us. "Selfie!" someone says, and we immediately start snapping photos. It feels celebratory, even necessary. We must document this episode of the story.

The elevator opens, and we're greeted by Senator William Monning, who initiated this event. He reached out to me months ago and made all the arrangements, along with Senator Ben Hueso and members of the California Latino Legislative Caucus. It's all come to fruition. We trail behind Monning, past the walls adorned with portraits of bygone decision makers. He leads us to a small room adjacent to the Senate floor. We're not prepared for what we're about to find on the other side of the door. It opens and immediately we're swallowed up by a crowd; photographers snap photos, hands reach out to us, politicians jockey, suits and perfume abound, the families are immediately accosted, and we're all separated in the excitement of this strangely orchestrated occasion.

⁂

They want to know where it all began. They ask questions, and then they stare at me for answers. They are relentless. "What made you want to go searching in the first place? How did this all start?" Their recording devices are on, notepads flipped open, at the ready. They don't want the long answer, they want a soundbite, a story to tell.

"There are too many beginnings," I say.

"Then give us one."

"You'll have to read the book."

They chuckle, jot down notes. I step away to find my children. I spot them at the reception table, salivating over a boat of colorful fruit, cuts of meat, and exotic flowers. All of which come from these very farmlands. The ones their grandparents and great-grandparents have worked. And the ones the passengers killed in Los Gatos Canyon also worked. Salvador already has a plate spilling over with grapes. He grins at me with all the pride a nine-year-old boy can muster.

A moment later, Senator Monning pulls me aside. He tells me, "Joan Baez was able to make it." He points toward a door. "She's in there warming up."

"Joan Baez is behind that door?" I ask.

He nods enthusiastically and begins to usher people out of the room. Only a few reporters and his constituents stay behind. Still, the room is chaotic with conversation. A minute later, I'm talking with Ofelia Treviño when a hand grabs at my wrist. I turn and find Joan Baez standing, holding my hand. She goes in for a hug. The whole room silences, turns to look at her. At us. More photos.

"I'm honored to meet you," I say.

"The honor is mine," she replies. "Thank you for the work you've done."

I hand her a signed copy of my book. She holds it to her chest. "Thank you."

Photos are being snapped as Joan makes her way around the room greeting everyone. She shakes my parents' hands, and they are beside themselves.

Soon the room is cleared out, and it's just us and Joan. The families of the passengers killed in the plane wreck at Los Gatos Canyon, and one of the folk-music icons who has kept this history alive. Her guitar magically appears. She strums it. And right there, in that tiny room, for just the few of us, she sings "Deportee (Plane Wreck at Los Gatos)." This is the first time Joan has sung the song for the very people it was written for. The only musician to ever do so. There isn't a dry eye in the room.

And now it's time.

Senator Monning guides us swiftly through a labyrinth of hallways. Joan has her arm threaded through mine, and she whispers into my ear, "Let's see where these halls will lead us." It's all surreal. I'm out of my skin, trying hard to stay focused on my purpose for being there. But in this instant, the excitement is electric, and it all feels like an illusion. We arrive at two large wooden doors. People in suits are eyeing us. The doors open to the Senate chambers—

There's a video of this moment online. I'm glad because if I wasn't able to see this, I would not be a credible keeper of this story.

The room is red. White columns everywhere. The video opens with Senator Ben Hueso addressing the chamber about the history of the plane crash. Meanwhile, we are all being ushered in behind him. At twenty seconds, to Hueso's right, Jaime Ramírez is the first to appear, with his wife Lilia at his side. He's holding the photo of his grandfather Ramón Paredes González. Next, Joan Baez steps forward with Rosa María, the niece of passenger Francisco Durán Llamas. Next is my son, Salvador, and then me. The rest of our group is ushered to the right side of the screen. And then my mother and father appear next to me. As Senator Hueso continues to address the chamber, Salvador stands in front of me, and I place my hand on his shoulder. I reach for Rumi, but she's at the far end with everyone else. We listen as Senator Hueso explains the events of January 28, 1948.

Senator Hueso: "The government made no effort to release their identity. They made no effort to communicate the tragic event to their families. And they made no effort to relocate the remains of these victims to their native country. To add insult to injury, they were buried in Fresno's Holy Cross Cemetery, listed only with the numbers one through twenty-eight, each number followed by two handwritten words, *Mexican National* . . . Tim Hernandez did the work that the government should have done, but seventy years later. And I'm honored to be able to take a moment to acknowledge this tragic event and properly memorialize the victims once and for all. And to let their families know how they will be remembered as a valued part of the history of our state. I'd like to introduce our majority leader and ask him to properly recognize the plane crash victims not represented here today by sharing their names."

Senator Monning steps to the microphone. He asks that everyone remain silent as the names are being read aloud. You can hear a pin drop. He stares down at his sheet of paper, begins—

Miguel Negrete Álvarez . . .
Tomás Aviña de Gracia . . .
Santiago García Elizondo . . .

Between each name Monning pauses briefly for effect. After the third name is called, I hear Salvador whispering something. I nudge him. At exactly 5:02 on the video, at the bottom right of the screen, you can see Sal whispering. What you won't see is me nudging him. A stealth parental tactic. Monning continues.

Rosalio Padilla Estrada . . .
Bernabé López García . . .
Salvador Sandoval Hernández . . .

In the space between each name, Salvador continues to whisper. Again and again, I nudge him. But all eyes are on us, and I'm hoping he'll just stop. At 5:19 you see Senator Hueso lean over to Sal and tap his shoulder. Joan glances over at Sal too. But Sal grows bolder. Another name is called, and I hear him clearly now. I recognize what he's saying. And I don't know whether to quiet him or join him. But it's too late. They've heard him. Another name comes, and Sal whispers again, *Presente.* My nine-year-old son is calling the dead into this space. Another name. *Presente,* he says to himself, to the air. He looks around, innocently. *Presente,* he says again. Some in the room strain to hear what the boy is whispering.

Severo Medina Lara . . .	*Presente*
Elías Trujillo Macías . . .	*Presente*
José Rodríguez Macías . . .	*Presente*
Luis López Medina . . .	*Presente*

At this point in the video, Salvador raises his voice, and you can now hear him clearly. *Presente!* But what you can't see is that the politicians in the room are beginning to stand. *Presente!* Sal says, encouraged by this. *Presente,* we all say, following Sal's lead. Another name. *Presente!* we call out. It builds.

Manuel Calderón Merino . . .	*Presente!*
Luis Cuevas Miranda . . .	*Presente!*
Martín Razo Navarro . . .	*Presente!*
Ignacio Pérez Navarro . . .	*Presente!*
Román Ochoa Ochoa . . .	*Presente!*
Apolonio Plascencia Ramírez . . .	*Presente!*
Alberto Raigoza Carlos . . .	*Presente!*

The entire Senate floor is now standing. *Presente!* They join in. The room fills with our collective voices. *Presente!* we say together. With each name I begin to envision the faces that go with it. *Presente!* I picture Celio Sánchez Valdivia's eyes in this moment, the little boy who lost his big brother. *Presente!* I see Casimira López's face, the young woman who lost her fiancé Luis. *Presente!* I glance over at Ofelia Treviño and her mother, who lost their tío Tomás. *Presente!* Jaime and Lilia Ramírez have tears in their eyes, as they hold up the photo of their tío Guadalupe and grandpa Ramón. *Presente!* Lisa and Rosa María hold their uncle Francisco's photo up proudly. *Presente!* And I think of all the families in Mexico. Don Fermín and his children, and all the kind people of Charco de Pantoja. *Presente!* My own mother and father, and my grandpa Alejandro and grandma Magdalena. *Presente!* And, of course, uncle Virgil. *Presente!* I grip Salvador's shoulder, look at my children. *Presente!* With each name, the spirits of our collective past are invoked into these chambers; all of them are here with us now. *Presente!* We know this. We feel this. *Presente!* We call out to them, and they come. We say their names, loudly and unapologetically. *Presente!* We call to them. You have not been forgotten. We could never forget you. You are all here with us now! *Presente!*

Guadalupe Hernández Rodríguez	*Presente!*
María Rodríguez Santana	*Presente!*
Juan Valenzuela Ruiz	*Presente!*
Wenceslao Flores Ruiz	*Presente!*
José Sánchez Valdivia	*Presente!*
Jesús Santos Meza	*Presente!*
Baldomero Marcos Torres	*Presente!*
Frank Atkinson	*Presente!*
Bobbie Atkinson	*Presente!*
Marion Ewing	*Presente!*

48

A LETTER TO YOU, MY CHILDREN

The ghosts of past, present and future stay with me . . .
Perhaps my calling is to tell a tale of workers on the land and
the story of the silent hands . . . One day, I too will become a ghost.

—DAVID MAS MASUMOTO, *LETTERS TO THE VALLEY*

SUMMER IS now over. I've just picked you up from visiting your mother in California, and we are again driving back to our home in El Paso. To view this interstate from a moving vehicle is to run your finger along the cartography of our growth. We've driven this desert more times than we can count. Memorized the landscape. For most people it's a two-day stretch. But not us. We make it in one. A sixteen-hour road, before sunrise to after sunset. The day goes from purple to blue to pink, back to purple. We greet each constellation by its name.

Passing Blythe, it occurs to me why it is that *they* have, several times now, entered my room and coaxed me out into the night. And why it is, when I am at the top of my porch, standing alone at the witching hour, that I am overcome with an immense sense of peace. Why it is that when I look up, I do not tremble at these same stars as Chita once did, in this very desert. Perhaps it's for the same reason that Maria, the niece of Alberto Raigoza Carlos, now works for an airline company and is unafraid of flying. Or why María Rodríguez Santana's nephew Mike now teaches inner-city youth about historical erasure and boldly advocates for immigrant rights. Perhaps we—the survivors of—are brought back to what were once spaces of grief, fear, or trauma for our family, and by our ability to triumph inside of these spaces, we become their redemption. As if to say, We are no longer afraid. We belong here.

ୄ

One day, when you are both adults, you will find yourselves on this route, perhaps individually or at different times, and it will all come rushing back. The conversations. The rest stops. One moment after another. But for now we are in the parenthesis. The purr of the road has you both asleep. Your trust in me is frightening. I don't blame my grandfather Alejandro. I cannot control what the road holds. Only that I hold on to the road. A horse trailer passes us, and for a brief moment I consider waking you both up to look at the horses. I decide not to. The wind slaps their faces and they look sad. I project emotions upon everything because everything is alive. Horses included.

I will never forget the story of the prehistoric horse told to me by don Miguel Pérez back in 2015, and how the community was left feeling duped by the paleontologists. I remember the frustration I felt at the blunt assignment don Miguel had given me that day. The last thing I needed was responsibility for locating something I had no interest in finding: horses. Ancient horses at that. And yet, seven years later, I would locate the horse, and its caretaker, Dr. Óscar Carranza Castañeda, and in our conversation he would never once mention the promise to return the horse to the people of Charco de Pantoja. To this day the fossil sits inside la Universidad Nacional Autónoma de México. It's only now that I'm remembering a quote I once heard on a podcast: *The fossil is not the animal. The fossil is not the bones of the animal. The fossil is the stone's memory of the bones of the animal.* And it begins to make sense. Maybe what don Miguel was suggesting I find was not the animal at all. Nor the bones of the animal. Maybe what he was suggesting that day had more to do with the memory of the animal. Maybe the Horse Story was a kind of parable, or an hechizo, cast just a few hours before I was to leave Charco de Pantoja indefinitely. Maybe it was his way of saying: *Whatever stories you have taken from here—bring them back.*

ୄ

The door is permanently open now, and *they* know where to find me. But I will continue to search. Until the families of all thirty-two passengers are found. I'm aware that this will take a lifetime. The search is intermittent. As much as possible, I am trying to remain present for you both. And for myself. It's too easy to be distracted by the pull of other gravities.

It is said that your great-grandmother Magdalena, with only a tenth-grade education, once wrote a letter to President Kennedy about the mistreatment of veterans, namely her husband. Whether or not Kennedy responded, who knows. When I first began this search in 2010, Barack Obama was still in his first term as president, and he was deporting people at a higher rate than any president before him. I thought of my grandmother. Here I was—two writing degrees—and it never occurred to me that writing a letter might be an effective tool. I had to try. We must always try. I wrote the president a letter, asking him to reconsider the inhumane impact of his immigration policies. *Dignity.* That was the word I used. I invoked my grandmother's name. My letter was met with a computer-generated response. I've saved the correspondence for you in our family archive. The one you both make fun of. But one day you will be the guardians of these boxes. And you will find yourselves reaching back to touch the objects and ephemera, evidence of the love you come from.

I wrote that letter eight years before we would learn of a place called Tornillo, Texas, where children were being incarcerated and detained for decisions and circumstances beyond their control. No child should be made to pay for their parents' choices. And yet, every day they do. We do. You do. It was an invitation to ask myself, In what ways have my own actions caged you? In what ways have you paid for the decisions I have made? Decisions born from wounds that I have both inherited and created. And for how long?

When I began to search for the families of the plane crash victims in December of 2010, Salvador, you were just two years old, and Rumi, you were six. You are now both teenagers, fifteen and nineteen. In this time, your universe has changed. You've lived in three different states and nine different houses, and attended nine different schools. They will say the instability has affected you. And they are right. But make no mistake, all of it was by design. I wanted you both to know that you belonged in all circles, in all spaces. From some of the most impoverished places in this country to the most affluent, you have sat at these tables and broken bread. Earth is your birthright. And your responsibility. *Everywhere you go is home.*

But no place more so than this desert.

Our beginning.

This is why when I learned that Tornillo was just forty-five minutes away from our front door I loaded you both into our car and we drove there with no real plan but to witness. And we did. That day two INS buses filled with invisible children, boys and girls your age, drove past us into the gates of the detention center. We could see the silhouettes of their heads staring out the windows at us. Something didn't feel right. We were a family, standing outside the gates, free. They were not. We could go home at the moment we chose to. They could not. We were given signs to hold up by the others who were also there to witness. We stayed all afternoon. That evening, we drove home, mostly silent. Interstate 10 held our prayers. I thought of my grandfather Alejandro. I noted: *This landscape will take your children.*

Within days the detained children decided they would not wait for any government system to recognize them. We will recognize ourselves, they silently agreed. Children inherently know the value of their own names. To kill the time, they had been given soccer balls—the official sport of Latin America. It didn't take long before they intentionally began kicking the balls over the fence to get the attention of those protesting outside the gates. On soccer balls they had written their names and the countries they were from: Guatemala, El Salvador, Mexico. On soccer balls, they told us: We are here. We are present. And these are our names.

Children.

We cannot wait for systems, or authorities, or people in power to restore our dignity or take heed of our humanity. We cannot rely on the hope that they will one day *see* us. I think of the poet-activist Audre Lorde, who famously wrote: *The master's tools will never dismantle the master's house.* And she is right. This business of dignity and seeing one another, it will only ever come from us. On soccer balls. On headstones. In songs. In books. In the way we treat one another. And in the stories we tell. What I have come to learn from this journey is this: a single story shared with another is medicine, but multiple stories shared in community is transformation. These are but some of the tools. They belong to you. Take them. Build.

෴

As we drive through Tucson, I'm reminded now of Alejandro's last days at the VA hospital here. How they were spent denying love. Denying he had any children at all. Denying himself the ability to love, and to be broken by love, once more. I want to mend my grandfather's wounds. Right here, right now: I want to tell you, my children, something you have heard me say a million times, though never before in this context. When I say these words to you, know that these are the many-layered stories I am speaking from—

In the past, I love you.

In the present, I love you.

In the future, I love you.

ര

The road is a repetition of itself, and yet you arrive elsewhere by the end of it. In this way, it is forgiving. The road is a chance to try again.

Let me rewrite this:

Why is it that I brought you kids back to this dusty landscape, where your great-grandparents experienced intense trauma and grieved until their dying day? The place that makes your grandmother cringe any time she has to set foot here for more than twenty-four hours. One way to say this is that I brought you here. Another way to say it is that *they* brought us here. And where is *here*?

It's no mystery, here is where your great-grandfather was defeated in single fatherhood. We can hear them whisper: What good is a father who cannot protect his children? Not even from himself. But like the road, we are forgiving. We offer the chance to try again. Just as you and your brother have circled back once more into our lives, so too has the circumstance. It's in this very desert that I have come into my own as a father. Your father. And I would not be this man if not for the enduring resilience and relentless love of your grandmother and grandfather. I intend to succeed. By which I mean, cultivate a sense of balance for you. By which I mean, be present with you. And I try and honor all sides of who I am. Of who we are. Man and woman simultaneous. It does not need a name. Call it love. We do what we must here in these borderlands, at the precipice of two countries, deep within the braid of our origins: Texas, New Mexico, old Mexico. Best believe our ancestors were resourceful people. They knew how to make the most with very little. And it's because of this that I know one thing for certain: Not only did they give us the wounds, but they have also given us the remedy. Their story is the medicine, administered only when we are ready to receive it.

෴

We are almost home.

You are now both awake, and I'm feeling spontaneous.

Approaching Deming, I pull off the highway, onto U.S. 180 north, across the overpass your grandmother used to hide beneath as a child, and out past the spot where her little sister Tilly was hit by a car and killed at sixteen. But I don't mention this. I don't need to. I am determined to leave the past behind us. I take you kids to the City of Rocks. This is near Nan Ranch, where Danny said your great-great-grandfather, El Tejano, once worked. We pull up to the giant boulders and leap out, and you both begin climbing, never once looking back. I try and keep up. My parents brought Virgil here two weeks before he was killed. He stood at the top of one of these rocks and shouted, "I love you, New Mexico!" A red-tailed hawk circles over us, and I want to make meaning of it.

"Try and find us, Dad!" your voices call out, tethering me back to the present moment.

It's our favorite game here. Hide-and-seek. I shut my eyes, briefly. Count out loud, eleven, twelve, thirteen years. "Here I come!" I shout back.

I can hear Rumi giggling, clawing at the side of some immense stone.

"Oh, I already hear someone over here!" I holler. "I'm getting close! I can smell you!"

And both of you begin to laugh loudly. The truth is, some days I hope this search never ends. The space between us is always only temporary. Some days it is shorter. Sometimes longer. But always we return to one another. The searching is the love. "Here I come!" I climb up the stone and see Salvador scurry below. Rumi, you leap down too, and both of you begin to run. I give chase, and we go scrambling in and out of the rocks, laughing, loud and hard and unapologetic. And this is it. Our laughter. Our joy. We are the redemption our grandparents sought. A father and his children. I know now. It will be our joy that heals all that has taken place before us.

Me, Rumi, and Salvador, El Paso, Texas, 2024.

PHOTO ARCHIVES

1. My Family
2. Funeral Services and Memorial Headstone
3. The Descendants
4. Journal Entries (And Still They Come)

My Family

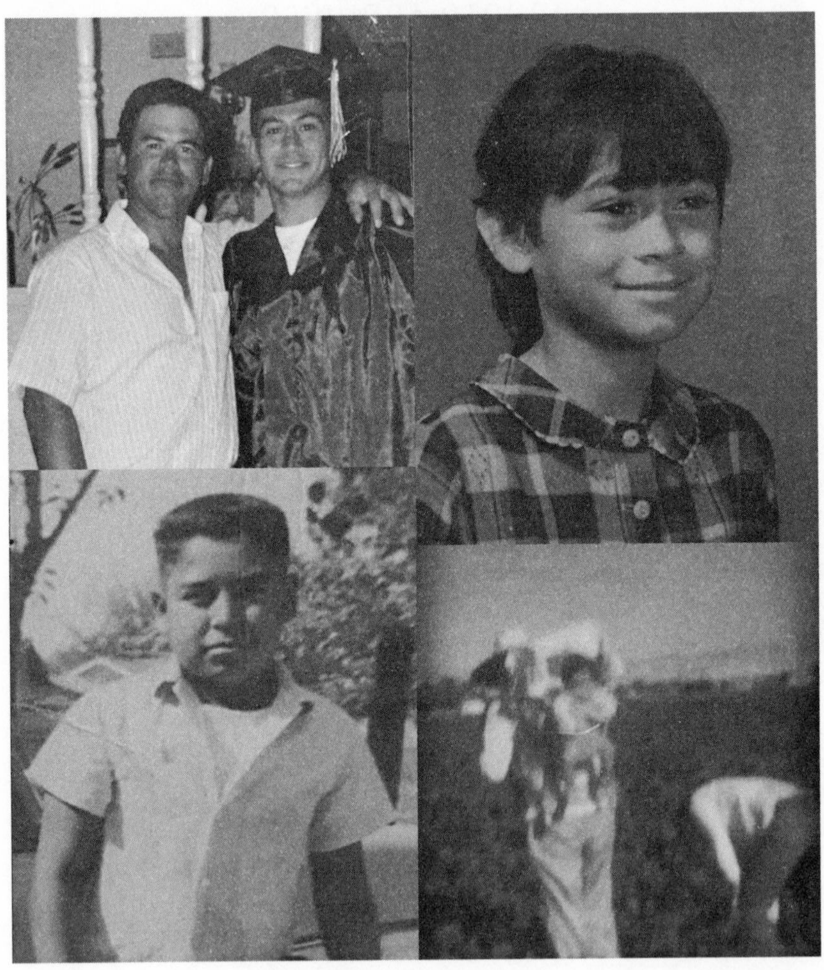

(a) Me with my uncle Virgil, 1992. (b) My mom, "Chita," Roma, Texas, 1960. (c) My dad, Felix Jr., farm labor camp, circa 1965. (d) Me, on my dad's back in the fields, Wyoming, 1975.

Funeral Services and Memorial Headstone

(a) Funeral services, Holy Cross Cemetery, 1948. (b) Close-up of caskets at the funeral services, 1948. (c) At the gravesite when I first began, 2010. (d) Installing new memorial headstone, 2013.

The Descendants

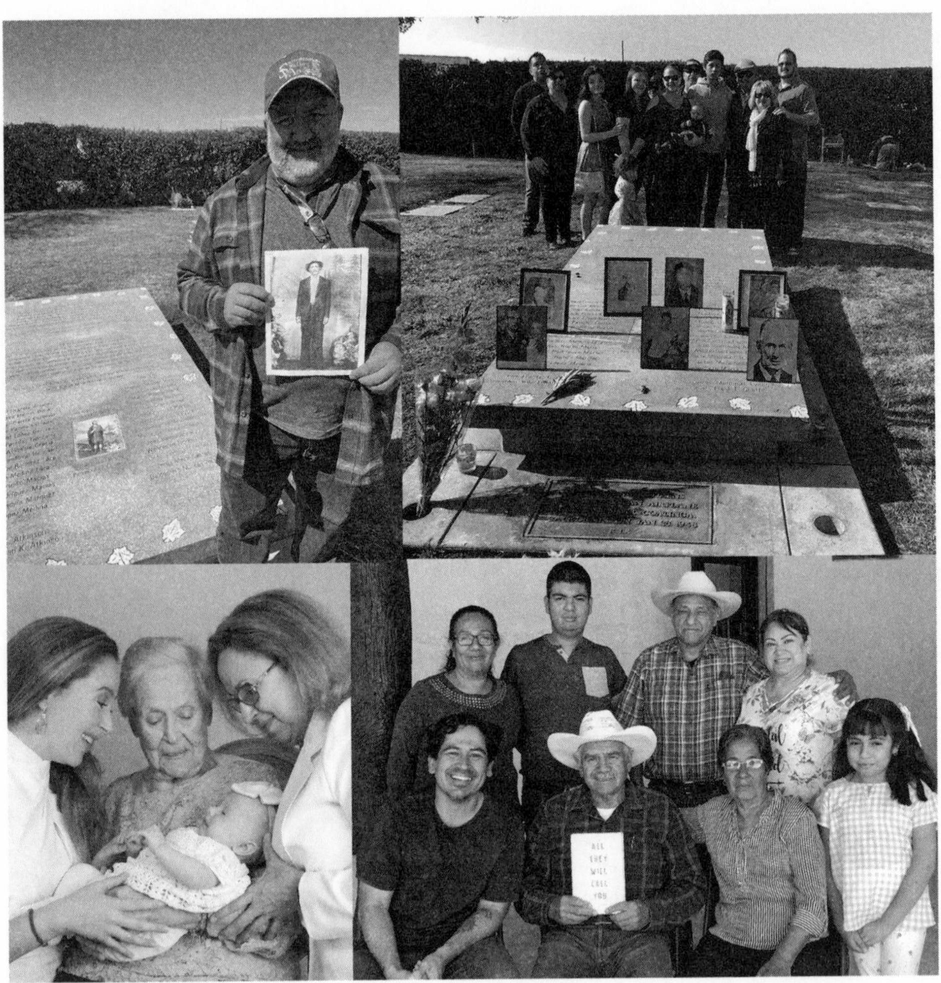

(a) Luis Estrada Andrade with his grandpa Rosalio's photo. (b) The family of María Rodríguez Santana. (c) The family of Tomás Márquez Padilla. (d) The Ramirez Lara family, Charco de Pantoja, Guanajuato.

Journal Entries (And Still They Come)

1/14/22

Its January again, the season of their arrival. Its no coincidence that most of the families have come to me at the beginning of the year more than any other time. Most of them in January, the month they were killed. the month of their exit. Just as I was finalizing the last draft of the book, I got a message through social media from a man named Luis Carlos Estrada Andrade. He says he's the grandson of passenger Rosalio Estrada Padilla. He lives in Bakersfield, just an <u>hour</u> from my parents house. He sent me a photo of Rosalio, or "mi abuelo Chalio" as he calls him, and Chalio's wife Concepcion. They're standing side by side. Luis doesnt know the year the photo was taken. He told me, "I am an immigrant, I want you to know." Promised him I'd look into this, but not today. The book is done. I'm done. For now at least. Have to get back to my life. To my kids. To my own heart. I want to live again in the present moment.

3/6/22
Was contacted today by another family. A young woman named Roxana Flores wrote to me from Atlanta, Georgia. Her great grand father was passenger Jesus Meza Santos. She sent me a photo of him. Jesus is wearing a white suit, and he's standing behind his wife, Amparo. Its a beautiful portrait. But again, I had to break the news to her that I won't be doing the research to confirm her claim. Not right now. I just can't. Rumi graduates high school soon, and Sal is moving on to 8th grade. And I need to get back into Dad mode again. Need to stay focused.

3/27/22

I had to! Roxana kept sending me info about Jesus, so I had to at least just take a quick peek. I found a record. Unlike anything I've ever found so far! Its a Death Registry but the story it tells isn't like anything I've seen before. The mexican officials arrive to the home of a widow. They tell her things. There are witnesses. The details are so compelling that I feel them wanting to pull me back in. But I can't. I just can't. I know what they're trying to do. This is how they work. This is their season. So, I spoke to them directly tonight. Explained how they'll have to wait. How my loyalty is first to the living. Life beckons. I must move on. Note to future self:

PHOTO CREDITS

x Photo of crash site. Source unknown, 1/28/1948.

xvii Photographs of the author's grandparents used with permission from the Hernandez and Zuñiga families.

23 Salvador Yeo Rodríguez. Stills from video taken by Peter Cannon in 2008. Used with permission of Peter Cannon and the family of Salvador Yeo Rodríguez.

27 Alberto Raigoza Carlos with niece Ofelia Morales, circa 1946. Used with permission from Ofelia Morales.

36 Letter from Alberto Raigoza Carlos to his sister Carlota, 1/3/1948. Used with permission from Ofelia Morales.

40 Tim with family of Alberto Raigoza Carlos, Mexico City, 2019.

49 Bea Franco, August 2013, Long Beach, CA. Used with permission from the Bea Kozera Estate.

54 Bea Franco with daughter Alicia Coronado, circa 1950. Used with permission from Alicia Coronado and the Bea Kozera Estate.

79 Community of Charco de Pantoja working to unearth the horse fossil found in 1990. Photo used with permission of Jaime Ramírez.

97 Author's mug shot, issued in Tulare County, 1993. Used with author's permission.

128 María Rodríguez Santana, circa 1947. Used with permission of the Rodríguez Santana family.

149 *El Faro*, Spanish-language independent newspaper, 3/1/1948, with permission from Jaime Ramírez.

153 Postcard photo of Laura and L. D. Nelson lynching from Highway 56 bridge in Okemah, Oklahoma, 5/25/1911.

170 Stills from raw footage taken by local news network on the night of Virgil's death, 5/18/1995.

197 Family of Apolonio Plascencia Ramírez, circa 1952. Used with the permission of the Plascencia family.

221 Manuel Corona Maynes, "El Tejano," and his wife Nicolasa Flores, with a baby, Columbus, New Mexico, circa 1912. Photo used with permission of the family.

227 Stills from video of the California State Senate recognition ceremony, 1/29/2018, Sacramento, California. Photographs of Joan Baez and families in gallery used with the author's permission.

235 Photo of the author with his children. Used with author's permission.

238 Photo Archives 1–4. 1: My Family. Photos used with permission of the Hernandez and Zuñiga families. 2: Funeral Services and Memorial Headstone. Photos used with author's permission. 3: The Descendants. All photos used with permission of the families. 4: Journal Entries: And Still They Come. Images used with the author's permission.

251 Author photo by Rumi S. Hernandez.

ACKNOWLEDGMENTS

FIRST AND FOREMOST, my endless gratitude to the families who continue to trust me with the telling of their stories throughout this project, specifically: To Jaime and Guillermo Ramírez and the Ramírez/Paredes/González/Lara clans in Charco de Pantoja, Guanajuato, whom I consider family, and with love to the memory of don Leovardo Ramírez Lara (RIP) To doña Ofelia Morales, Maria Guadalupe Cerecero Gutiérrez, Ivonne Cerecero Jensen, Xóchitl Cerecero Morales, Dr. Salvador Cerecero Morales, doña Elvira Perjuan Morales (RIP), and their beautiful family in Mexico City and Acapulco. To Ofelia Treviño, I'm so grateful to you, your mother, and your grandmother for your ongoing support. To Mike Rodriguez III, whose fearless voice echoes throughout this work, and to his family, Mike Rodriguez Sr., Sandra Andrade, Gonzalo González, and the whole Rodríguez and Santana clan, my endless gratitude, and to the beautiful spirit of Eugenia R. Andrade (RIP). To Luis Carlos Estrada Andrade and his family in Bakersfield, our search continues, mi hermano; and to Roxana Flores and her family in Atlanta, Georgia. To Rosa María and Lisa for your patience and understanding. To Kelly Coultier, Peter Cannon, and the family of Salvador Yeo Rodríguez, my gratitude. To the descendants of Beatrice Renteria Kozera (née Bea Franco), my dear friends Al Franco, Patricia Leonard, and Alicia Coronado, and in loving memory of Bea's great-granddaughter Alyssa Aileen Mendoza (6/27/99–1/3/21, RIP), who was gone far too soon but remains a beacon of light for her family.

To my children, Rumi and Salvador, this map is for you both, always for you. And for Quetzani Montaño-Sevilla, my beautiful child-in-spirit, thank you for the love and light you bring to me and your siblings, and to this world. To my parents Felix and Lydia Z. Hernandez, a brown boy could not have been any luckier than to have you both as gentle guides in this lifetime; thank you for teaching me what the love of a parent looks like. Thank you to my sister Delylah and brother-in-law Jason, and my nieces Destina Unica and Dezyrae Amor, for always having my back. And to my cousins Manny and Loretta Casillas, Thomas, Wanda, and Manny Jr., and their families, for the endless prayers, and for reminding me that El Paso is home. And to my cousin Nicky Casillas in Deming, NM, for being one of the keepers of our family's archives, I am grateful. To the memory of my cousin Rosalinda Galaviz (RIP), my aunt Emily Zuñiga (RIP), and my aunt Apolonia Flores Maynes Casillas (RIP). My literary familia, a small tribe of supporters: Juan Felipe Herrera and Margarita Luna Robles—I will thank you 'til the end of times; Daniel Chacón, Jason McDonald, Kalina Gallardo, Ser Godoy, Bill and Mary Anna Clark, and Literarity Bookstore—you are all home to me. Also, a deep bow to my brilliant colleagues and students at the University of Texas El Paso Department of Creative Writing for having my back. The final draft of this book was finished while on faculty leave in the spring of 2022, and with support from a UTEP Career Enhancement Grant in the summer of 2021, and I am grateful to both selection committees for finding value in this project. Big shout-out to *Words on a Wire* on KTEP 88.5 FM for giving me a space to hone my interview skills on radio and cast great stories out across the borderlands. Also, my gratitude to the following organizations, institutions, and individuals who have championed this work over the last thirteen years and counting: the Woody Guthrie Center, Deanna McCloud, Kate Blalack, Nora Guthrie, Anna Canoni, Woody Guthrie Publications Inc., Arlo Guthrie, Sarah Lee Guthrie, Joan Baez, Joel and Lauren Rafael, War Eagles Museum, El Paso–based pilot Steve Johnson, Carlos Avila and Elaine Montalvo, Poets & Writers Inc., Senators Bill Monning and Ben Hueso and the California Latino Legislative Caucus, Juan Esparza, reporter extraordinaire, Carolyn Caldera, Jean Luc De Fanti, Steve Ayala, Diane and Bill Vigeant, John Boomer and Maggie Billiman, Johnnie "Babs" Sherlock, Jake and Karissa Yeager, Nancy Birdwell, Lee Scazighini, Carlos Castillo, the staff at the R. C. Baker Museum, Dr. Juan Garcia and Josie Rangel and the Fresno

State Chicano Alumni Book Club, and journalist Gustavo Arellano, thank you all for your ongoing support.

So much love to those who walked with me, listened to my stories, offered feedback, or held my hand through various parts of this journey: Estela and Cory Sue, Norma Gonzalez, Felix Duarte, David Herrera, Tony Delfino, Eliseo Carrera, Mayela Padilla, Alessandra Narváez Varela, Luis Humberto Valadez, Kimberly Castillo, Dayanna Sevilla, Daniel Grandbois, Alfredo Corchado y Angela Kocherga, Laurie Ann Guerrero, Angela Anderson Guerrero, Ana Saldaña, Jesse Julian Vera, Sam Sanchez, and Alejandra Huerta. A special shout-out to the ones who've recently passed and were a part of my support team in the early stages: my cousin Arturo Garcia Jr. (RIP), my godfather Fred Bueno (RIP), and my homey Raoul "El Charro" Hernández (RIP), whose big voice and beautiful songs accompanied many of these stories in live performances.

Also, a deep bow to the musicians and performers whom I've been privileged to collaborate with on various staged productions/performances of these stories: Lance Canales, Joel Rafael, John Boomer, Johnny Irion, Coco Alcazar, Raoul "El Charro" Hernández, Sunday Iris, Ana Saldaña, Richard Montoya, Mark "Silent Bear" Holtzman, the legendary David Amram, Will Kaufman, Carlos Rodriguez, Elena Holly Klaver, Richard Juarez, and Ted Nunes. I'm sure I've forgotten a few more, but to you my sincere apologies. Om mani padme hum.

ALSO BY TIM Z. HERNANDEZ

Nonfiction

All They Will Call You

Fiction

Mañana Means Heaven

Breathing, In Dust

Poetry

Some of the Light

Natural Takeover of Small Things

Culture of Flow

Skin Tax

ABOUT THE AUTHOR

Photo by Rumi S. Hernandez.

Tim Z. Hernandez is an award-winning writer, multidisciplinary artist, storyteller, and research scholar. His work includes poetry, novels, nonfiction, screenplays, and staged productions, and his writing and research have been featured in the *Los Angeles Times*, the *New York Times*, C-SPAN's *Book TV*, and NPR's *Latino USA*. He is the recipient of numerous awards, including the American Book Award for poetry and the International Latino Book Award for historical fiction, and in 2018 he was recognized by the California State Senate for his work locating the victims of the 1948 plane wreck at Los Gatos Canyon. Hernandez holds a BA from Naropa University and an MFA from Bennington College. He is an associate professor at the University of Texas El Paso's bilingual MFA program in creative writing, and he currently lives in El Paso, Texas, with his two children. You can find more information at his website, www.timzhernandez.com, and follow him at @t.z.hernandez.

THEY ARE STILL OUT THERE (THE LIST)

Guadalupe Rodríguez Hernández, padre Guadalupe Rodríguez, Mexico City

Ignacio Navarro Pérez, padre José M. Navarro, Rancho Cerrito, Michoacán

Santiago Elizondo García, padre Valentino Elizondo, Ocotlán, Jalisco

Luis Medina López, padre Daniel Medina, Morelia, Michoacán

Manuel Merino Calderón, padre José Merino, Puebla, Mexico

Juan Ruiz Valenzuela, padre Jerónimo Ruiz, Nochistlán, Zacatecas

Wenceslao Flores, padre Jerónimo Ruiz, Nochistlán, Zacatecas

Salvador Hernández Sandoval, padre Jesús Hernández, Jalpa, Zacatecas

Tomás Aviña de Gracia, madre Rosa Mercado, Tepic, Nayarit

Baldomero Torres Marcos, padre Martín Torres, Mexicali, B.C.

Elías Macías Trujillo, padre Juan Macías, Ensenada, B.C.

Bernabé García López, Magdalena, Jalisco

Román Ochoa Ochoa, padre Román Ochoa

José Macías Rodríguez, Manalisco, Jalisco

Severo Medina Lara, Huanusco, Zacatecas

Miguel Álvarez Negrete, Puebla, Mexico

Martín Navarro Razo, La Barca, Jalisco

Marion Ewing, Balboa Park, California